# CAR MASCOTS

# CAR
# MASCOTS

AN ENTHUSIAST'S GUIDE BY
Giuseppe di Sirignano and David Sulzberger

Crescent Books · New York

# Acknowledgements

THE AUTHORS AND BLACKER CALMANN COOPER LTD. would like to thank the owners of car mascots illustrated in this book for allowing them to be reproduced: James Baron (Plates 34, 80, 81, 83, 139, 201, 211); the Etro Collection (Plates 10, 35, 38, 42, 49, 50, 58, 67, 73, 87, 91, 100, 102, 120, 121, 127, 146-149, 151, 152, 158, 169, 170, 177, 178, 181, 190, 192, 196, 197, 206, 212); Minas Kachadurian (Plates 20, 33, 63, 70, 74, 75, 90, 94, 97, 160, 161); Casa Agnelli (Plate 28); Peter Ritchley (Plates 4, 15, 53, 56, 57, 60, 61, 142, 144, 145, 153, 192); Mario d'Urso (Plate 31); Frederico Sofio (Plates 98, 202); Museo dell'Automobile, Turin (Plate 46); the Beaulieu Motor Museum (Plate 137). They are also grateful to the following for providing photographs: Christie's, South Kensington (Plates 13, 43-45, 48, 66, 77, 79, 85, 89, 91, 99, 128, 179, 205); Christopher Vane Percy (Plates 131, 134, 140, 179); Coy's (Plate 75); the Imperial War Museum, London (Plate 165); l'Automobiliste (Plate 157); Autocar (Plates 7, 17, 134, 207, 208); Kobal Collection (Plate 54). The authors would like to thank Patricia Garnett for her assistance in writing the book.

This book was designed and produced by
Blacker Calmann Cooper Ltd, London

Library of Congress Catalog Card Number: 77-76555

This edition is published by Crescent Books
a division of Crown Publishers Inc.
by arrangement with Blacker Calmann Cooper Ltd.

Printed in England

# Contents

1. Carved and painted wooden figure from a nineteenth century Swiss sleigh.

# 1
# THE EARLY
# YEARS

The Tortoise beat the Hare! They were well matched but the road narrowed once the hare lost its lead and there was no further chance to overtake. The tortoise was French, made of amber-coloured smoked glass, mounted on the radiator cap of a handsome Delage. The hare, upright ears gleaming, was English and was made of silver-plated bronze. He stood atop the imposing radiator of an Alvis. This unlikely race took place fifty years ago.

These two fabled animals were car mascots. Along with an endless menagerie of other real or imaginary beasts and a truly cosmopolitan crowd of miniature figures of people, they were the decorative ornaments that crowned radiator caps on the hoods or bonnets of automobiles. They are also known as hood ornaments and radiator mascots. In French the common terms are *Mascottes* and *Bouchons de Radiateurs*.

Why were they there? What real need was there for these often gaudy and distracting figures? Mechanically they had no *raison d'être*, but they played a singular and vital role: they added a personal touch to cars. A glance through this book will show car mascots embodying every possible human aspiration, superstition, hope, fear, expectation, pretention and obsession as well as man's sense of fantasy and humour. By the time prehistoric

man first invented the wheel he already had a highly developed sense of symbolism. From earliest times, when man's urge to communicate through decoration inspired wall-painting in caves, symbols have been chosen for specific purposes. Individuals, families, places and nations all have their symbols.

Mascots are symbols of this sort, but they also serve two additional purposes. They bring their owner luck and distinguish him from other owners. Thus a mascot becomes a constant companion and, in travel especially, a guide. Since ancient times boats and vehicles have had such mascots: the figureheads that guide ships' bows through the oceans and that lead antique sleighs through the snow are the direct precursors of car mascots. Like them they were most often figures of animals or people, real or imaginary; their wide eyes saw the way, while they embodied the spirit of the ship to which they frequently gave their name. Similarly as roads improved and coaches and carriages became more common and their design more standardized a need developed to distinguish between them, so the owner's monogram or coat of arms was frequently mounted or painted on.

When Howard Carter discovered Tutankhamun's tomb in the November of 1922 and, in it, the greatest archaeo-

2. A falcon, bearing an image of the sun on its head, from Tutankhamun's chariot.

3. An imitation of the sun-crested falcon on Tutankhamun's chariot. U.K., 1920s. Chrome-plated brass, $4\frac{3}{4}$ in (12 cm).

logical treasure ever found, the imagination of the entire world was immediately captured. Among the many priceless objects buried with the child king was the earliest-known mascot made for a wheeled vehicle: this is the sun-crested falcon mounted on the Pharaoh's golden chariot to guide him on his last journey to the other world, more than three thousand years ago. This was an obvious model for car mascots and virtually exact copies can indeed be found on several English cars of the 1920s.

Ever since cars first appeared on the road owners have used them to express their individuality. There is no need to be an expert on Freud to know immediately that the owner of a tomato-red car has a different character from the owner of a sober grey or blue one. In recent years racing stripes and all sorts of stickers such as the ubiquitous smiling yellow circle and Snoopy, the Beagle, have been painted or stuck on cars to make them different from others. In some countries, particularly the U.S.A., 'Vanity Plates', the licence of one's choice, frequently with the owner's nickname or initials, make a car stand out. In the early days of motoring, car mascots were an ideal way of making oneself and one's car distinctive.

Though they continued in Europe until the 1940s and in the U.S.A. until the 1950s, most car mascots were produced in the first three decades of this century. They clearly show the influence that artistic movements had on contemporary taste and reflect successive trends in design and the impact of different schools—traditional, decorative, functional, realist, aerodynamic, *Art Nouveau, Art Deco, Moderne Style,* and Cubism. Moreover, car owners in this period, regardless of whether their taste was traditional or avant-garde, were invariably wealthy and their cars like their yachts signified their membership of an elite. On these early machines the mascot was a further distinctive mark, clearly reflecting the owner's taste.

Car mascots fall into three categories:

*Custom Mascots*: these were the mascots commissioned by a client from a particular artist (such mascots are often signed and unique), or were small sculptures issued by the artist in a strictly limited edition, often designed specifically for cars. Others that fall into this category were constructed or adapted by the owner himself to suit his own particular requirements.

*Fantasy Mascots*: as cars became more popular and the demand for mascots increased, an industry developed which mass-produced them. These vary greatly in quality and include every sort of human and animal figure, as well as commemorative and promotional designs.

*Company Mascots*: these were the mascots which were (and in some cases still are) provided by car companies. Rolls Royce's 'Spirit of Ecstasy' is the best known example.

4. This is one of the few Italian mascots and was made for Garavini, a firm of coachbuilders. The globe is inscribed 'Cerozzeria E. Garavini & Co. Torino' and 'Fond. Lagana Napoli'. Italy, late 1920s. Chrome-plated bronze with blue enamel on the globe, $5\frac{1}{4} \times 7\frac{1}{2}$ in (13.5 × 19 cm).

5. 'The Spirit of Triumph' mounted on a moto-meter; created by F. Bazin, one of the most important French mascot designers. This mascot was often copied and influenced designs such as Packard's 'Goddess of Speed'. France, 1920s. Silver-plated brass, 7 × 5 in. (18 × 13 cm).

It is not possible to pinpoint precisely when the first car mascot was made. In 1827, when the motor car was still a fantasy, an English inventor designed a steam-powered three-wheel carriage called the 'Docudep'. The drawings show a figure of a golden bird with outstretched wings, perched on the tiller bar; although the Docudep was never produced, this is probably the first instance of a mascot being installed on a 'motorcar'. Figures of St Christopher, the patron of travellers, were such an obvious choice for hood ornaments that they could be said to be the precursors of mascots. When John Scott Montagu, later Lord Montagu of Beaulieu, created a sensation by driving to the House of Commons in 1899, he also established the idea of mascots by sporting a statuette of St Christopher on his radiator cap. One of the earliest English mascots designed as such, a winged wheel, appeared in 1908 on Jack Johnson's Austin Grand Prix racing car, and

by 1910 several mascots were available in shops selling motoring accessories. The first Rolls Royce 'Spirit of Ecstasy' appeared in 1911 and was shortly followed by the Vulcan 'Blacksmith'. The first American mascot was 'Gobbo', the god of good luck, designed and copyrighted by L. V. Aronson in 1909. He also designed many other mascots including the 'Speed Nymph' in 1910, a figure of a diving girl which became the model for so many nymph mascots and was immediately widely copied on both sides of the Atlantic. A mascot commemorating the opening of the Panama Canal was patented and shown in 1913 at the great San Francisco Exhibition. By this time car mascots were being featured regularly in car advertisements and had become firmly established as common motoring accessories.

Among the first car mascots, and probably one of the causes of their invention, were moto-meters or calormeters which were introduced in the first decade

6. The earliest British company mascot, a winged wheel, on Jack Johnson's 1908 Austin Grand Prix racing car.

## It's illuminated!

HERE is the latest Benjamin contribution to "Motoring with an easy mind." The difficulty hitherto experienced, on some cars, of easily reading the temperature indicator at night, is dispelled by the new illuminated Boyce Motometer.

A small lamp of negligible consumption, concealed in the top of the instrument frame, diffuses an even and pleasing light down the tube, giving the appearance of phosphorescence, and providing an ever visible indication of engine temperature, even on the darkest road.

Wiring is extremely simple and unobtrusive, suitable lighting cable and full directions being supplied with each instrument.

For use on either 6 or 12 volt car lighting circuits, and in two handsome designs—the Radio model at 42/-, and the De Luxe model (as illustrated) at 63/-.

*Send for Leaflet No. 1036.*

## ALWAYS IN THE LINE OF VISION —VISIBLE BY DAY OR NIGHT

### THE NEW ILLUMINATED BOYCE MOTOMETER
### MOTOR HEAT INDICATOR

RADIO **42/-** MODEL

DE LUXE **63/-** MODEL

THE BENJAMIN ELECTRIC LTD., Brantwood Works, Tottenham, London, N.17.

7. An advertisement in the *Autocar* of July 19, 1929; the radiators of early cars frequently boiled over and so moto-meters, which kept the driver informed of the engine's temperature, were popular.

of the century. These fascinating and necessary devices kept drivers constantly informed of the temperature of their radiators which, especially in the early days of motoring, were likely to boil over at any moment and were constantly in

8. Moto-meter or calormeter 'with outspread wings attached'. U.K., 1920s. Brass, $3\frac{1}{2} \times 4$ in (9 × 10 cm).

need of refilling. By 1917 there were eighteen million moto-meters in use on trucks and cars in the U.S.A.

Mounted on radiator caps, the glass faces of these circular devices were sometimes engraved, the gauges decorated and frequently wings were attached to their stems. At this time many mascots were so designed that they could be fitted directly on to a moto-meter. The two best known manufacturers were Wilmot-Breedon in England and Boyce in the U.S.A. By the 1930s most cars had temperature gauges on their dashboards, though some mascots with thermometers were still made. For instance, in 1934 a Ford Greyhound could be purchased with a thermometer tucked between its rear legs.

The invention of the automobile was very quickly followed by the creation of automobile clubs. These issued badges for their members which were frequently attached to the radiator cap and mounted as mascots. The most famous of these in Britain, the A.A. and R.A.C., remain unchanged today; the Automobile Club de France also had a mascot designed round its initials. There are photographs which show that as early as 1905 an A.A. badge was mounted as a mascot on a Talbot; these badges sometimes stood alone and sometimes were attached to a moto-meter.

9. Moteur Club de France mascot; as automobile clubs became fashionable, mascots which advertized the owner's membership became increasingly common. France, c. 1920. Nickel-plated brass, $3 \times 3\frac{1}{2}$ in (8 × 9 cm).

Many mascots between 1910 and 1920 were lucky emblems. The reason for their popularity is clear; the driver was dealing with a machine that could go wrong, and even become dangerous, so many car mascots were little idols to pacify those various mysterious influences that affected the traveller. From the very beginning there was a healthy fear of cars—a feeling which was sometimes reflected in their mascots. The very idea of the horseless carriage was terrifying, and the tremendous noise and horrible accidents that occurred confirmed many people's belief that cars were infernal monsters terrifying law-abiding folk and causing havoc by making carriage horses bolt. At the outset of motoring, legislation was passed in many countries which stated that cars had to be preceded by a man on foot waving a lantern or a red flag, or ringing a bell to warn the unsuspecting of its immediate arrival.

Good luck symbols appeared in the shape of devils, imps, pixies, gnomes, as well as St Christopher, to ward off the evil eye and mitigate the unforsee-

10. Nymph holding a skull. France, *c.* 1915. 6 in (15 cm).

able disasters that were the result of driving. These varied from country to country. In England, for example, there were black cats, a good luck symbol there, although in Latin countries they are the opposite. There were also figures of jokers, hunchbacks, the lucky swastika, and a number of death symbols, such as the skull and crossbones. A sinister French mascot called 'Hara-kiri' appeared in 1913 depicting a Japanese gentleman disembowelling himself.

Another consequence of the invention of the automobile was the traffic police-man, who was drafted into existence to sort out the congestion and accidents that cars created. Figures of these police-men became very popular as mascots in the early days of motoring; between 1910 and 1914 dozens of models appeared, some of them realistic and some satirical; serious representations include a 'copper' clearing the way for a car to travel down the road, his hand outstretched to halt cross traffic. A similar policeman was available with arms which twirled around independently in the wind as the car picked up speed. The best known

11. 'Rigoletto'. A lucky hunchback. Italy, early 1920s. Nickel-plated brass, $5 \times 1\frac{1}{2}$ in (12.5 × 4 cm).

12. 'Bobby', signed 'J. Hassall'. U.K., 1911. Silver-plated brass, 4¾ in (12 cm).

13. (*opposite, above*) A child wearing a policeman's helmet, holding a large stopwatch in one hand and indicating to the traffic to stop with the other. Made by Elkington and signed 'Vernon May'. U.K., 1907. Silver-plated brass, 4¾ in (12 cm).

14. (*opposite, below*). Policeman, U.K., *c.* 1910. Nickel-plated brass, 3½ × 2 in (9 × 5 cm).

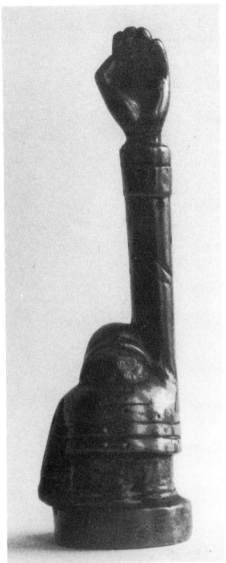

15. 'Stop', a caricature of a policeman. U.K.,
c. 1915. Silver-plated bronze, 7 in (17.5 cm).

caricature was John Hassall's Humpty
Dumpty-like 'bobby' whose helmet and
egg-shaped head could be twisted into
any position.

There have always been humorous
and satirical mascots, but these were
especially popular in the earlier days
of motoring. In addition to caricatures
of policemen, pedestrians and soldiers,

16. 'Bécassine', the head of this mascot is spring-mounted. France, mid 1920s. Silver-plated bronze, 5 in (13 cm).

such comic characters as Mickey Mouse appeared. In the 1920s a figure of 'Puss in Boots' holding a mouse by the tail in his right paw, was particularly popular.

The invention of the car was swiftly followed by the first aeroplanes and often the first motorists were pioneering

18. Mickey Mouse, inscribed 'Produced by consent of Walter E. Disney'. U.K., mid 1930s. Chrome-plated bronze, 5½ in (14 cm).

pilots and flying enthusiasts as well. By 1911 it was possible to find several miniature model planes to mount on the front of one's car. These sometimes had revolving propellors and were among the first mascots with independently moving parts.

In the first two decades of this century, a new form of international rivalry developed. Countries competed to establish new land speed records, and great endurance races such as the Paris–Peking

17. An illustration from an *Autocar* of 1934 showing Mickey and Minnie Mouse Mascots. U.K., 1934. Enamelled bronze and chrome.

19. 'Gnome' aero-engine mascot. U.K., *c.* 1912. Brass, 9 in (23 cm).

20. 'Sans Moteur', a flying snail. France, early 1920s.

Europe, and the resulting nationalist sentiment felt by patriotic citizens in all countries influenced mascots and provided a new *raison d'être* for them. Mascots were created to inspire support for soldiers and national defence; even in the U.S.A., which did not enter the war until 1916, mascots reflecting sup-

rally were organized. Cars became symbols of national prestige and early car mascots often reflect this. An excellent example is a six and a quarter inch high brass standing figure of 'Britannia' with a scroll at her feet, on which is inscribed 'Plenty for all'. One hand rests on an anvil, the other holds a horn of plenty and the base is inscribed 'I have resolved to purchase British Empire Productions; all British campaign'.

The outbreak of World War I in

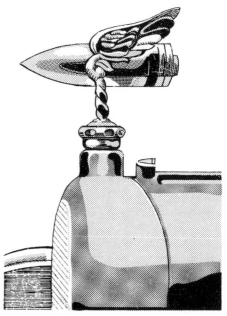

22. Lloyd George's car mascot, a winged shell. U.K., 1915.

21. Uncle Sam riding a shell. U.S.A., 1918.

port for the Allies appeared. Patriotic emblems abounded: in England there was Britannia and the lion of the Empire, in France the cock and Marianne, and in the U.S.A. Uncle Sam and the American eagle.

One patriotic mascot showed the figure of an English 'Tommy' crushing a helmeted Prussian eagle beneath his foot, closely paralleling representations of St George and the Dragon. Lloyd George's car had a winged artillery shell mounted in 1915. Old Bill, a well-known comic character, was England's favourite cartoon figure during the Great War. There were many mascots of him, and

23. Mono-plane
with the French
Air Force insignia
in enamel; signed
'F. Bazin'. France,
early 1920s. Silver-
plated brass and
enamel, 3¾ in
(9.5 cm) long.

24. A British soldier bayoneting the
German Imperial eagle, mounted on part of
a shell casing. U.K., 1915. Brass, 4¼ × 3 in
(11 × 8 cm).

25. Britannia, this mascot was advertized
in a contemporary catalogue as costing
ten shillings. U.K., 1913. Nickel-plated
brass, 3¾ × 2½ in (9.5 × 6 cm).

today one occasionally sees him on the hood of cars in England, showing that the owner is a veteran of the Great War. In France, Renault, which played an important role in the French war effort and made the taxis in which French soldiers were driven to stop the German Blitzkrieg at the Marne, put a miniature tank on its cars to commemorate the tank that it built for the French army.

A type that appeared during World War I was the photo mascot; these consisted of small glass-fronted lockets in which were photographs of heroes, leaders and generals, such as King George V, Kitchener, Jellicoe and Joffre. Another symptom of patriotic feeling, so strong at this time, was that many radiator caps were equipped to carry flags. After the war patriotic mascots, for instance the helmeted and begoggled head of Lawrence of Arabia, continued to be popular.

26. 'Lion Rampant'. U.K., 1910. Brass, $4 \times 3\frac{1}{2}$ in (10 × 9 cm).

27. A head and a figure of 'Old Bill', designed and signed by Bruce Bairnsfather (1888–1959) who served in France in World War I and was famous for his war-time cartoons. U.K., 1919. Bronze, $3\frac{1}{4}$ in ($8\frac{1}{2}$ cm) and $4\frac{1}{4}$ in (11 cm) high.

# 2
# CUSTOM
# MASCOTS

In the early years of motoring nearly all mascots were custom made, mostly in the *Belle Epoque* styles of the late nineteenth century. In France, the famous *Animalier* school of bronze casters which had made the large sculptured animals popular throughout the nineteenth century, began producing mascots, and so in France most custom-designed mascots, and even many of the more commercial fantasy mascots were signed by the artist. In Germany it was fashionable to install the family coat of arms or heraldic device in silver or bronze on a car's radiator; these mascots were made to order, and represent a continuation of the emblems that had traditionally appeared on coaches.

By the 1920s not only was there an enormous variety of subjects for mascots, but because of the equally varied artistic styles, the same subject, for example the figure of a woman or a bird, could be found treated in a multitude of different ways. Catalogues of this period show any number of nymphs in various stages of undress, hundreds of animals and many humorous figures.

After World War I, peace, and the international conferences that attempted to make this peace permanent, clearly

28. The Agnelli mascot, designed by Edoardo Rubino and given by the artist to Donna Virginia Agnelli, the wife of the head of Fiat, for use on her cars. Rubino (1871–1954), an Italian sculptor at the beginning of the century, was well-known for the monument he built to King Umberto I at Aosta and to Alessandro Vittoria at Trento. Italy, 1929. Silver, 7 × 3¾ in (18 × 9.5 cm).

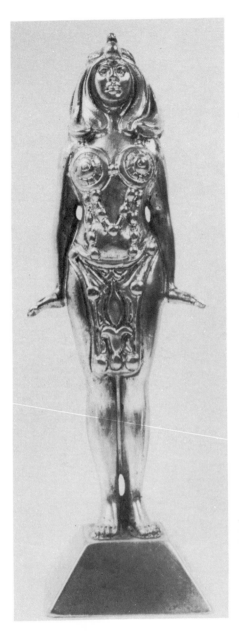

The taste for oriental art in the early 1920s can be seen in the car built in 1921 by the coach builder M. A. Stehr, of Levallois in the outskirts of Paris, on a Secqueville-Heyau chassis. This was a 'Coupé Boudoir', entirely decorated in the Japanese style. Its interior contained two separate seats and a removable settee, all upholstered in dove grey silk woven with a pattern of oriental flowers; the seats had gold lacquered wooden dragons as headboards, armrests and feet. The door panels and the dividing panel that separated the chauffeur from the passengers were also lacquered with a design of flowers and birds; the door handles and other indoor metal

29. (*Left*) Egyptian woman, signed 'Ellis', copyright A.E.L. U.K., early 1920s. Silver-plated brass, $7\frac{1}{4}$ in (18 cm).
30. (*Below*) A seated sphinx. U.K., c. 1918. Silver-plated bronze, $5\frac{1}{4}$ in (13.5 cm).

influenced fashion. A new optimism, after four years of austerity, and a new international awareness of the art of other cultures had a tremendous effect on taste. The various styles of Victorian art were superseded by orientalism, paganism and exotic fashions; imitations of Egyptian and African art became the vogue.

31. (*Above*) The Fokker mascot, signed 'Annie Cottrau'. This mascot was designed by Annie Cottrau Fokker for the car of Tony Fokker, the Dutch plane builder. The model for the winged boy was Alessandro d'Urso, the artist's nephew. Italy, 1923. Platinated bronze, 5 × 4 in (13 × 10 cm).

32. (*Below*) An armorial mascot, the torso of a winged unicorn holding a shell. U.K., *c.* 1915. Silver-plated brass, 4½ × 5½ in (11.5 × 14 cm).

33. (*right*) 'La Folie de la Vitesse', signed 'P. de Soete' (1886–1948) and inscribed 'Bien Amicalement à M. Verdyck'. This mascot was awarded a prize at the 1921 Salon de l'Auto in Paris. Belgium, 1921. Silver-plated brass, 6½ in (16.5 cm) high.

fixtures were imitation oriental bronzes. An antique Japanese chest with gold inlay was installed as a liquor cabinet; this was fitted with crystal bottles and glasses engraved with oriental motifs. As the name 'Boudoir' implies, several mirrors were installed in the passenger compartment reflecting the light of a Japanese-style ceiling lantern. Outside, the conservative bodywork of the car gave no hint of the Asiatic splendour within. The only echo of the interior was the mascot: a plump figure of Buddah astride a mythological monster.

The discovery of Tutankhamun's tomb in November 1922 awoke interest in Egypt, and as a result the treasure of the Pharaohs had enormous influence on European taste. Hair styles, hats, jewellery (especially the popular, new costume jewellery), furniture and entire

interiors appeared in imitation of the objects found in Egyptian tombs; it was a fashion that affected the population as a whole, not just the elite. Car mascots were also influenced. The Stutz Company in America chose Ra, the sun god, as its symbol and in England Armstrong-Siddeley mounted sphinxes on their cars; in France Rolland-Pilain used a winged sphinx. The art of Africa also had a significant impact in Europe, where the Benin bronzes were particularly admired. Primitive art was considered pure and unencumbered by external influences, an idea which preoccupied such artists as Modigliani and Brancusi. A derivative school, *Art Negre*, developed and objects of all sorts, including car mascots, were produced in this style.

34. (*right*) Mascot of two motorists' heads in the *Art Negre* style. France, early 1920s. Glass, $5\frac{1}{2}$ in (14 cm).

35. (*Below*) A woman holding a shooting star. U.S.A., early 1930s. Chrome-plated brass, $5 \times 7\frac{1}{2}$ in ($13 \times 19$ cm).

36. (*above, left*) A figure of an officer. U.K.,
*c.* 1915. Silver-plated brass, $8\frac{1}{2}$ in (22 cm).

37. (*left*) A seated girl, signed 'M. Gouraur'.
U.K., early 1920s. Silver-plated brass,
5 × 3 in (13 × 7.5 cm).

38. (*above, right*) A pilot's head. France,
late 1920s. Silver-plated bronze, $6\frac{1}{4}$ in
(16 cm).

39. (*bottom, right*) An anchor, U.K., early
1920s. Brass, $4\frac{1}{2}$ × 5 in (11.5 × 13 cm).

40. 'Standing elephant, signed 'L. Maurel' and inscribed 'Andron Fondeur'. France, 1913. Silver-plated bronze, 4 × 5½ in (10 × 14 cm).

41. Jumping horse and jockey, signed 'A. Guillaume'. France, late 1920s. Silver-plated bronze, 5½ × 5 in (14 × 12.5 cm).

In the later 1920s another influence on decorative art came from the 'New World'. Brazil and South America were brought into the public eye by Colonel Fawcett's exploration of the Amazon, his disappearance and Peter Fleming's recovery expedition. The nationalization of British oil interests in Mexico and the frequent revolutions in Latin American countries focused attention on that Continent. Pre-Colombian art became very fashionable and there developed

42. The crouching figure of a winged man, an example of the 'Aztec' style. U.S.A., early 1930s. Chrome-plated bronze, 5 in. (13 cm).

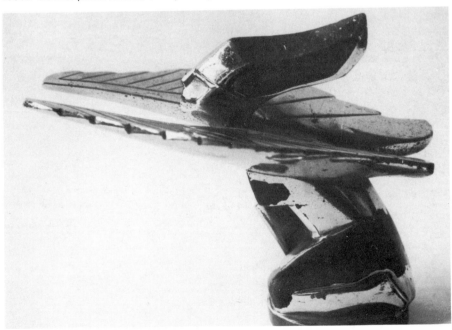

43. This model cine-camera was sold in 1975 at Christies for £360, a record price for metal mascots at the time. U.K., 1920s. Silver-plated brass, 4 in (10 cm).

The cinema was as significant an influence as ballet. Stars of the silent screen such as Theda Bara, the quintessential 'Vamp' (her exotic name is an anagram for 'Arab Death') were portrayed in metal, the figures appearing as lamps, ornaments and, of course, car mascots. Famous film stars frequently bought magnificent motorcars. Valentino's Knight-engined Voisin car had a coiled cobra as its mascot; Gary Cooper's Duesenberg had a running lady and one Hollywood movie mogul had an English silver-plated model of a cine-camera. In 1930 the great director, Alexander Korda, made a spectacular musical called 'Lilies of the Field'; in it a 'ballet mécanique' had dancers impersonating wheels, cylinders, electrical components and various other pieces of machinery, and in its most ostentatious tableau, Corinne Griffith, the star, crowned a temple-size car grille, a live mascot standing on a giant radiator cap.

a contemporary derivative, commonly known as the 'Aztec style', in which architecture and decoration echoed the shapes of Mexican pyramids. Some car mascots also emulated pre-Colombian figures. Exotic stars, such as Mata Hari, the famous war-time spy, performed oriental dances in fantastic, scanty costumes; Isadora Duncan, the nymphlike American dancer, was preoccupied with the fluidity of movement and created her own interpretations of the style of classical Antiquity; the influence of these women on contemporary taste can be seen in the statuettes of nymphs and female figures so successful as mascots at the time.

Ballet was extremely popular in the first two decades of this century, and had an impact on public taste which was reflected in fashion and art. In 1924 Diaghilev's *Ballet Russe* produced Poulenc's 'Les Biches'. This ballet influenced an entire generation of designers and created a new style of female beauty, relating it to the grace and elegance of animals; gazelles and antelopes became a prominent feature of the decorative arts, frequently appearing as mascots. The Singer car company called one of its models the Gazelle.

44. Kneeling girl. U.K., early 1920s. Nickel-plated bronze, $3\frac{1}{4}$ in (8 cm) high.

45. Boar's tusks. U.K., late 1920s. 8¼ in
(21 cm).

46. 'Rien ne sert de courir' ('It is no use
running'); the tortoise and the hare are at a
winning post, inscribed 'BUT' ('goal').
France, 1911. Bronze, 5 × 3¼ in (13 × 9 cm).

47. Shivering nymph, signed 'Becquerel' and
stamped 'Etling Paris'. France, mid 1920s.
Silver-plated bronze, 6½ in (16.5 cm).

48. Left: This statuette of a bulldog, which
has a real leather collar, was not originally
designed as a mascot but was mounted as
such by its owner. France, 1920s. Chrome-
plated brass, 4¼ in (11 cm).
Right: This figure of Shu Lao, holding a
scroll, was mounted on a radiator cap in the
1920s. China, nineteenth century. Pewter,
5 in (13 cm).

Another strange cinema personality, Ohn Maung, the Burmese producer, had mounted on his Vauxhall a truly bizarre beast which had the head of an elephant with stag's antlers on the body of a rearing horse.

Kitsch, a word coined to denote the degradation of art to the very lowest common denominator of popularized taste, is the term most often used today to describe much decorative art from this period. In addition to the more splendid prototypes, the 1920s saw the mass production of cheap objects in metal, ceramics and that new material, 'plastic'. With the mass production of automobiles came the mass production of mascots, many of them perfect examples of 'Kitsch'.

As a reaction against such useless decoration, movements such as the *Bauhaus* sought to create inherently simple designs and set artists technical problems in an attempt to reach the ideal of a practical aesthetic. The riveted aluminium Voisin mascot, the winged-'Cocotte', was an attempt, albeit humorous, at creating an ornament appropriately mechanical in style.

A group of five Futurist mascots of this period are of great interest being first class examples of modern sculpture. Designed by Joel and Jan Martel, two brothers who were both well-known sculptors, these were cast in bronze and chromed. Each one is different and they were ordered for the cars of various well-known people, like Robert Mallet-Stevens, the architect and designer, the Sizaire brothers, owners of the automobile company, Gabriel Voisin, the car designer, and the architect, Le Corbusier. These and several other mascots, including a fine silver-plated bronze rabbit by Becquerel, a sphinx by R. Sertorio in silver plated bronze with an ivory face, and several examples of Lalique's glass mascots, have been shown in Europe and

49. Girl holding a dove, signed by 'Henry Arnold' and stamped 'Susse Frères, Paris'. France, early 1920s. Bronze, 8¾ in (22 cm).

the U.S.A. in exhibitions of the arts of the 1920s. In England, Ian Anderson commissioned Percy Metcalfe, the designer of the George Cross, to make a stylized, 'modern', running, Wildcat mascot for him, and Poiret, Paris's leading couturier, had a mascot specially created for his Hispano-Suiza by the sculptor, Goursal, in 1934.

In the 'twenties and 'thirties custom mascots for the few and fantasy mascots

50. This mascot was inspired by Houdon's 'La Frileuse'. U.K., early 1920s. Chrome-plated brass, 6 in (15 cm).

French mascots on the cars they supplied for export.

Even when the cars normally came equipped with a company-approved mascot, some coachbuilders removed these company mascots and substituted their own designs. For example, the beautifully streamlined model 1106 Packard that Le Baron produced in 1934 had neither of the two standard Packard mascots, but its own custom-designed comet-shaped ornament, one of the first of a type of streamlined mascot that was to become extremely common in the U.S.A.

As companies began regularly to supply mascots with their cars, and as a whole industry for producing mascots had grown up, the demand for custom-

51. This mascot of an embracing couple is reputed to have been made for a bookmaker in Leeds and to have been subsequently removed from his car by order of the town Watch Committee because it was considered indecent. U.K., late 1920s. Glass, 9 in (23 cm) high.

for the many existed together, and sometimes a particularly successful custom mascot was either reproduced or simply copied. Since most expensive cars of this time were delivered with engine and chassis by the manufacturer to a coach-builder of the purchaser's choice, many were subsequently fitted with a custom or fantasy mascot by the body's supplier. For example, a 1927 Isotta-Fraschini type 8A, bought for $18,500, by a New York foreign car dealer, Joseph Gaeta, and bodied by Fleetwood, the American firm, had a coiled snake mascot similar to Valentino's Voisin, as indeed did several Isotta-Fraschinis; others carried Bazin's 'Spirit of Triumph'. Mascots were never particularly popular in Italy and so Italian car manufacturers and coach-builders frequently installed English or

made mascots decreased sharply in the 1930s. Some were still made for special occasions such as royal weddings; European royal families continued to have their own personal mascots; in Britain, King George VI favoured the Imperial crown and lion, Queen Elizabeth the Queen Mother has Britannia standing on the globe whereas Queen Elizabeth II has St George and the Dragon. The Emperor of Japan continues to use a limousine, on which a silver chrysanthemum blossom is mounted as a mascot. Indian Maharajahs often had personal mascots on the cars in their extensive garages, and a few wealthy individualists and some eccentrics continued to indulge their fantasies.

One Rolls Royce owner ordered a 'Spirit of Ecstasy' in ivory for his car, while another having had a stainless

52. A figure of a girl, the initials 'M.O.' are inscribed on the base. This mascot was sold by the jewellers, Mappin and Webb. U.K., 1922. Polished brass, $7\frac{1}{2} \times 4$ in ($19 \times 10.5$ cm).

53. A bear holding the A.C. company emblem, in the centre of which is a three-penny bit, an English coin. U.K., late 1920s. Silver-plated bronze, $4\frac{3}{4}$ in 12 cm).

steel joint removed from his hip installed it in place of the company mascot; engraved on its base was the inscription 'A Loyal Supporter'. In America Jackie Coogan installed 'The Kid', a French bronze figure of a small boy with an ivory head; Mrs Corning, the glass heiress, had a glass figure of Pegasus, symbolic of her racing stables, mounted on the Rolls she kept in upstate New York.

Doris Duke had a silver 'Hawaian Surfer' on her Peerless car in Waikiki; an American art collector installed a cast of a small Rodin bronze, and some Texas cattle ranchers mounted long horns on the hoods of their cars. After World War II very few custom mascots appeared especially since the proud owner of a particular mascot would usually keep it and transfer it to his new model when changing cars.

54. Corinne Griffith as a giant car mascot in Alexander Korda's film, 'Lilies of the Field'.

# 3
# FANTASY
# MASCOTS

By the middle of the 1920s the mass production of car mascots had become an industry on its own, with several companies rivalling each other to produce mascots of all types and at every price-level. France and England were the leading producers. In France design competitions were held at motor shows and both there and in England these 'fantasy' mascots were well advertised and were available at most garages and motor-accessory stores. Many were made with separate wings or other moving parts, and some of those that are still available today have been in production, with vir-virtually no change, since they were intro-duced fifty years ago by these manufac-turers. An endless array of stylized figures and all sorts of creatures, real, imaginary or extinct, appeared in chromed bronze, enamel or glass. One English firm of mascot producers offered, in fine Anglo-Saxon tradition, ninety different breeds of dog, fifteen types of cattle, thirty-five horses, forty birds, and sixty other animals and fish, with kangaroos and kiwis for Australia and New Zealand.

Some of the many animals provided by fantasy mascots manufacturers were specifically designed for cars which did not sport a company mascot. A squirrel holding a nut (of the mechanical not

55. Three begoggled motorists by Jean Verschneider. France, c. 1915. Bronze. Left: 4¾ in (12 cm). Centre: 6 in (15 cm). Right: 5 in. (13 cm).

56. (*above*) A speed god, signed 'Lotti' and produced by Marvel. France, early 1920s. Nickel-plated bronze, 6 in (15 cm).

57. (*left*) A Lizard standing on a rock signed 'A. Rogé'. France, mid 1920s. Nickel-plated bronze, $4\frac{1}{4}$ in (11 cm).

the edible type) was produced for the Model T Ford. Animal names were popular for cars at this time and a mascot of the appropriate animal was often available, a leaping gazelle for the Singer Gazelle, a jaguar for Jaguar, a snipe for the Humber Snipe, a swift for the Swift, and so on.

The cost of mascots varied tremendously. An English catalogue lists mascots from a few shillings to several pounds; in it Lalique glass mascots were priced at five to six guineas. The most expensive mascot was an 'Illuminated Mercury-Pegasus', a silver-plated statuette of the god holding the winged

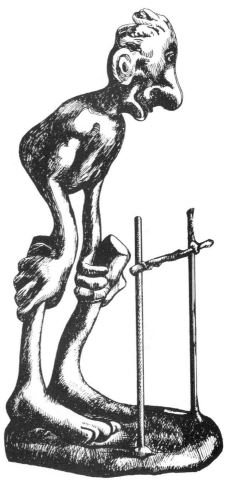

58. (*Above*) Squirrel holding a nut. This mascot was designed to be mounted on English Fords. U.K., 1920. Nickel-plated brass.

59. (*right*) 'Le Saut en Hauteur', this fantastical mascot was produced by Etablissements Marvel. It won ninth prize in the 1921 'Concours de Bouchons de Radiateurs' in Paris. France, early 1920s.

60. (*below*) A stylized bird fitted with a thermometer, signed 'Auscher' and inscribed 'Banville, Paris'. France, mid 1920s. Silver-plated bronze, 8¾ in (22 cm).

61. (*above*) A stylized head, signed 'Auscher'. France, 1920s. Chrome-plated bronze, $3\frac{1}{4} \times 5\frac{1}{2}$ in (8 × 14 cm).

62. (*right*) 'Amo', designed by 'Desmo', is described in a 1938 catalogue as being 'a mascot of beautiful proportion and a real art study; it maintains the usual Desmo high standard of accuracy and faultlessess; two sizes available; large size, each 35/-. Small size, each 17 6d'. U.K., late 1930s. Chrome-plated brass, 4 in (10 cm).

63. (*below*) Egyptian lady with trumpet. signed 'M. Giraud-Riviere'. France, early 1920s. Bronze, $5\frac{1}{2}$ in (14 cm).

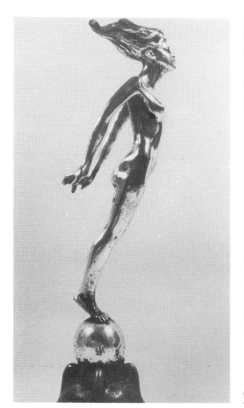

65. (*above*) Figure of a woman, U.K., *c.* 1917. Silver-plated bronze, 7 in (18 cm).

66. (*below*) Left: Kneeling nymph, signed 'Elie Ottavy'. France, early 1920s. Silver-plated bronze, 8 in (20 cm). Centre: 'L'Egyptienne', signed 'D. Alonza'. France, early 1920s. Silver-plated bronze, 8 in (20 cm). Right: 'La Sorcière'. France, early 1920. Silver-plated bronze, 7 in (18 cm).

64. This nymph is mounted on a Ford radiator cap. U.K., late 1920s. Chrome-plated bronze, 7½ in (19 cm).

67. (*above*) Right: This well-known and popular mascot. 'Speed Nymph' is still in production and has become the company emblem of the Louis Lejeune mascot manufacturers. U.K., 1916. Nickel-plated bronze, $6\frac{3}{4} \times 4\frac{1}{4}$ in (17 × 11 cm). Centre: Nymph on a car wheel. U.K., c. 1913. Brass, $6\frac{1}{4}$ in (16 cm). Left: 'Whirled along'. U.K., c. 1913. Silver-plated bronze, 7 in (18 cm).

68. (*left*) Mermaid. U.K., pre-1920s. Nickel-plated bronze. 6 in (15 cm).

horse in one hand and a torch lit with coloured bulbs in the other. Some of the most expensive could be bought at such jewellers as Mappin and Webb and Aspreys.

In the United States fantasy mascots appeared later than in Europe, although they were to last twenty years or so longer. Car radiators were placed beneath the hood or the bonnet of American cars, thus hiding the radiator cap, several years before this happened in Europe, and so the first mascots that were not attached to the radiator cap but merely fixed to the front of the car appeared on American cars. As a result, in the 1930s fewer of the European fantasy mascots were imported

69. 'Showman', the arms of this mascot were designed to revolve as the car moves. France, early 1930s. Chrome-plated bronze, 6¼ in (16 cm).

into the U.S.A. and American mascot producers such as Florman of New York, Ternstedt of Detroit, Jarvis of Grand Rapids and Stant of Connersville, designed ornaments that could easily be integrated into the over-all lines of the car and as streamlining became more popular so did streamlined mascots. By the end of the 1930s most American car mascots were provided by the company that built the car, although American accessory manufacturers continued to produce hood ornaments usually of the rocket type well into the 'fifties.

The tendency towards stylized and streamlined subjects became evident in Europe in the 1940s as well. Nymphs became more elongated, as if they were Olympic champions leaning forward in their search for speed, health and sunshine. The feminine figures of the early 1930s gave way to the more masculine figures of sportsmen. Humorous and mechanical figures disappeared, and among the few remaining mascots that had moving parts were small planes with two independently revolving propellors.

70. A butterfly, signed 'F. Bazin'. France, mid 1920s. Silver-plated bronze, 4¼ in (11 cm) and Icarus, signed 'F. Bazin'. France, mid 1920s. Silver-plated bronze, 6 in (15 cm).

These were provided to flying clubs for private plane owners with the registration number of the aircraft engraved on the wings.

The vogue for sporting mascots produced many designs of swimmers, tennis players (one popular French mascot shows the figure of Suzanne Lenglen, the French woman champion), football players, cricketers, skiers, jumping horses with or without their jockeys, golfers and flying golf balls. Sports associations and other groups often created their own mascots; for example, members of the R.A.F. had flying wings as car mascots, and there is a five inch long mascot of a leaping salmon inscribed 'Fly Fishers' Club'.

In addition to acting as indicators of social position and taste, car mascots were also used for publicity. Michelin created mascots in the form of Bibendum, the fat, be-goggled rubber-tyre man that was the firm's symbol. Kervoline, the lubricant firm, also had its own company mascot and Rudge-Wilworth, a

71. An R.A.F. mascot. U.K., 1930s. Brass, $10\frac{1}{4}$ in (26.5 cm).

72. Winged nymph on an aquaplane, riding a wave. U.K., late 1930s. Chrome-plated brass, 7 × 6 in (18 × 15 cm).

73. Left: 'Kick-off', an American football player. Made in U.K. for export to the U.S.A., early 1930s. Bronze, 7 in (18 cm). Centre: Girl Hurdler, U.K., 1932. Nickel-plated bronze, 3¾ in (9.5 cm). Right: Suzanne Lenglen, the French tennis champion. France, mid 1920s. Silver-plated bronze, 8¾ in. (22 cm).

74. Left: Horse and jockey, signed 'A. Renevey'. U.K., mid 1920s. Silver-plated bronze, 5 in. (12.5 cm). Centre: Cricketer, U.K., mid 1920s. Brass, 4½ in (11.5 cm). Right: Skier. U.K., early 1930s. Chrome-plated brass, 5 in. (13 cm).

wire-wheel company, produced as its promotional mascot a caricature monkey holding a wheel. The British Piston Ring Company introduced 'Miss Brico', a nymph holding a ring, symbolic of 'Symmetrical Perfection'. *Le Petit Parisien*, a newspaper, had its mascot on all its press cars: a winged globe in chrome with blue, red and black enamel, flanked by the letter P on either side. Sharpe's, the British manufacturers of toffees offered sweet-tooth motorists a caricature called Sir Kreemy Knut, while the Toffee-Manufactory of Stockport ordered a mascot of a squirrel for use on its vans to promote its 'Squirrel Horn' candy. 'Mr. Therm', the emblem of the British Gas Authority, also appeared as a car mascot. A special mascot of a soldier was designed for car owners among the theatrical group playing 'Journey's End'

75. (*left*) Dolphin, signed 'R. Camus' and inscribed 'Assurance tous risques auto London Guarantee and Accident Co, 3 rue Scribe, Paris IXᵉ'. France, early 1920s. Silver-plated bronze, 2 in (5 cm).

76. (*above*) 'Miss Brico', the British Piston Ring Company mascot.

77. (*below*) Mr Therm, the gas-flame sprite. U.K., 1930s. 4¾ in (12 cm).

I. British policeman and aviator, both designed by John Hassall (1868-1948).
U.K., 1911. Silver-plated brass, $4\frac{3}{4}$ in (12 cm) and $4\frac{1}{4}$ in (11 cm).

II. (*above*) A cat and a small boy, both made by Red Ashay. U.K., late 1920s.
Glass, 5½ in (14 cm).

III. (*below*) 'Grande Libellule', signed 'R. Lalique, France', late 1920s. Glass, 8¼ in (21 cm).

78. (*below*) Sir Kreemy Knut, a mascot promoting Sharpe's toffee. U.K., early 1930s. Chrome-plated brass, $5\frac{1}{2}$ in (14 cm).

79. (*right*) The mascot was used to advertise the play 'Journey's End'.

on its world tour. It was advertised as being obtainable to motoring admirers of the play from the stage manager of the Prince of Wales Theatre.

Among the most interesting 'fantasy' mascots produced were those made of glass. René Lalique, the French glass-maker, whose 'Liberty' style jewellery and objects were extremely fashionable, was at the peak of his popularity when he began to make car mascots; the first, a dragonfly with folded wings was intro-duced in 1915. Not all of the Lalique car mascots were originally designed as such, while others that were have since been given other uses. Some ornamental pieces and paperweights were the right size for a radiator cap and were adapted as mascots, others were specifically

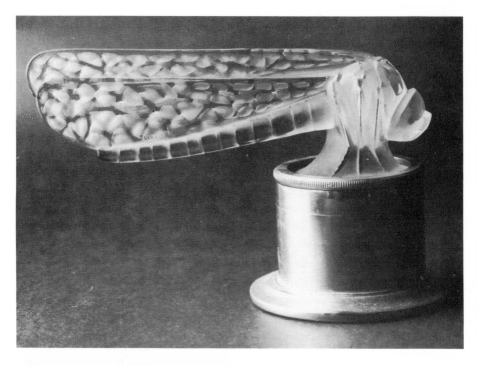

80. (*above*) 'Petite Libellule' on illuminating base, signed 'R. Lalique'. France, early 1920s. Glass, 6¼ in (16 cm).

81. (*left*) Stylized flying nymph, stamped 'L.B.'. France, late 1920s. Glass, 5 in (13 cm).

made to fit on cars, but today serve as decorative objects, paperweights or book-ends. Lalique glass was made to the highest standards obtainable using mass-production techniques; each piece, though machine moulded, was usually finished and polished by hand. The demand for Lalique mascots was high but they were so expensive to produce that profit margins were low and the company eventually stopped making them. Among the best known of approximately thirty mascots designed by Lalique is the large eagle's head; this fierce and imposing symbol of military might was chosen by Hitler as an appropriate gift for his military commanders and so can be seen in some photographs of war-time Mercedes-Benz staff cars.

Although less well known than Lalique, other firms produced glass mascots, such as Sabino and Etling in France and Warren Kessler and Red Ashay in England.

There were basically two ways of mounting a glass mascot on a radiator cap. The simplest was to fix the mascot directly onto a metal base which screwed into the radiator outlet, serving as the cap. Lalique devised a second, more complicated type which had a thicker cylindrical metal base in which there was a bulb that illuminated the mascot from below when the car's lights were turned on. This whimsical object could just be regarded as functional since theoretically

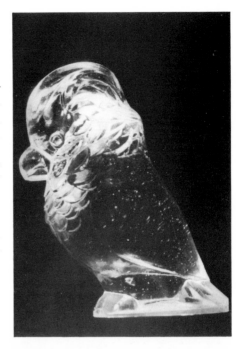

82. (*right*) Cockatoo, by Model. France, mid 1920s. Glass, 4½ in (11 cm).

83. (*below*) Shooting star, signed 'R. Lalique'. This mascot was illuminated by a light in the base. France, late 1920s. Glass, 2¾ in (7 cm).

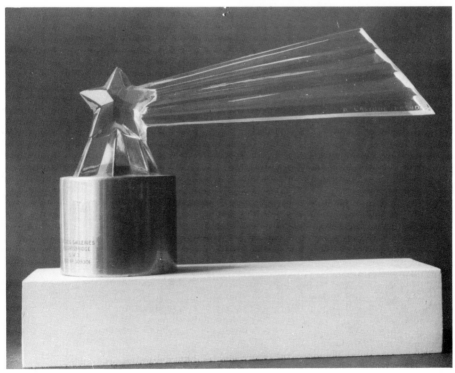

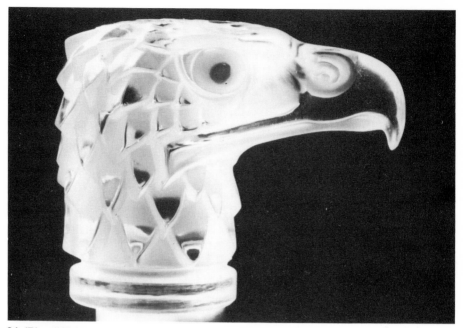

84. 'Tête d'Aigle', signed 'Lalique, France'. France, late 1920s. Glass, $4\frac{1}{2} \times 6$ in (11.5 × 15 cm).

85. Frog, signed 'R. Lalique'. France, early 1920s. Glass, $2\frac{3}{4}$ in (7 cm).

the mascot acted as a parking light. Sometimes coloured filters were installed between the bulb and the glass mascot, thus the colour of the mascot could be altered to match that of the car or a rainbow effect of different colours could be obtained. Such mascots immediately became popular, but were even more costly for Lalique to produce. As a result many cheaper copies were made, especially in the U.S.A. and Lalique withdrew from the field.

The Red Ashay company in England perfected such lighting systems by using a four-colour filter. The colours were changed manually or, alternatively, a sophisticated propellor system could be installed whereby the colours changed according to the speed at which the car was travelling. Red Ashay produced a number of exotic mascots with such names as 'Victorious', 'Spirit of Wind', 'Peter Pan', etc. which were immensely popular.

86. 'Victoire',
signed 'R. Lalique'.
France, early 1920s.
Glass, 2¾ in (7 cm).

87. Lalique's
trophy for the
'Côte d'Azur
Pullman Express',
signed 'R. Lalique'.
This is an example
of a mascot, in
this case Lalique's
'Vitesse', being
used as a trophy.
France, 1929.
Glass, 6½ × 6 in
(16.5 × 15 cm).

88. (*above left*) The club mascot of the Antideluvian Order of Froth Blowers. The barrel is inscribed 'No Heels Tap' on the back. U.K., late 1920s. Silver-plated brass, $4\frac{3}{4}$ in (12 cm).

89. (*left*) A caricature of a man, possibly of André Citroen, holding a pet model car on a leash, signed 'Sasportas'. France, mid 1920s. Silver-plated bronze, 4 in (10 cm).

90. (*above*) 'Speedy'. A running figure of an auto-mechanic in overalls holding a spanner. U.K., 1930s. Silver-plated bronze, $4\frac{1}{4}$ in (11 cm).

91. (*opposite, above left*) A motorist seated on petrol can and spare wheel. U.K., early 1920s. Brass, $4\frac{1}{4}$ in (11 cm).

92. (*opposite, above, right*) 'Nini'. signed 'Bertin'. France, early 1920s. Bronze, 3 in (8 cm).

93. (*opposite, below*) Fox, huntsman and hound, signed 'E. T. Mercier'. France, early 1920s. Silver-plated bronze, $4\frac{1}{4}$ in (11 cm).

94. (*above*) A stylized cougar. U.K., early 1930s. Chrome-plated bronze, $5\frac{3}{4}$ in (14.5 cm).

95. (*left*) 'Dinkie Doo', a character from a popular song. This mascot was available in polished brass or nickel-plated brass for thirty-two shillings and six pence. U.K., 1919. Nickel-plated brass, $5\frac{1}{4} \times 4$ in ($13.5 \times 10$ cm).

96. (*below*) Terrier's head, one of the few wooden mascots made, probably hand carved by a firm that produced umbrellas and walking stick handles. U.K., early 1930s. Painted wood with glass eyes, $2\frac{1}{2} \times 4\frac{3}{4}$ in ($6 \times 12$ cm).

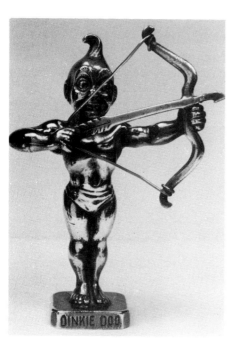

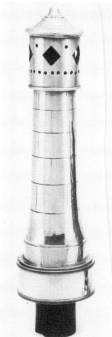

97. (*above*) Left: Bouledogue à la chaine', initialled 'G.E.'. This 'cubist' mascot won first prize at the 1930 'Concours de Bouchons de Radiateur' in Paris. France, 1923. Silver-plated bronze, 4 × 5 in (10 × 13 cm). Right: A 'cubist' hare. France mid 1920s. Silver-plated bronze, 5¾ in (14.5 cm).

98. (*below*) Trout, manufactured by A.E.L. U.K., early 1920s. Silver-plated bronze, 3 in (7.5 cm).

99. (*left*) This lighthouse incorporates the car's radiator cap and pressure valve. It also has an electric light which shone through the cellophane-fitted windows. U.K., mid 1920s. Nickel-plated brass, 8 in (20 cm).

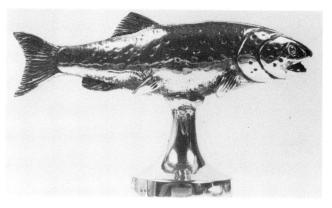

100. (*above*) Parrot. U.K., early 1920s. Enamelled bronze, 4 in (10 cm).

101. (*below*) 'The Bluebird'. U.K., 1910. Brass, 3 × 4¼ in (8 × 11 cm).

102. (*above, right*) Monkey holding a lamp, signed 'M. Le Verrier'. Four different Le Verrier monkeys were produced; this one had a coloured electric light bulb in the lantern. France, mid 1920s. Brass, 5½ in (14 cm).

103. (*below, right*) Pigeon. U.K., early 1920s. Silver-plated brass, 4¾ in (12 cm).

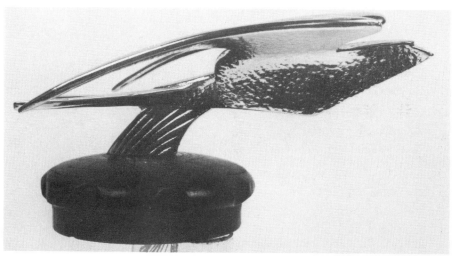

104. (*above*) Martin, made by Desmo. U.K., 1938. Chrome-plated brass, $2\frac{1}{2} \times 1\frac{3}{4}$ in (6 × 4.5 cm).

105. A cock, the symbol of France, standing on a wheel. This mascot is associated with the 'Automobile Club de France'. France. 1920s. Bronze, 6 in (16 cm) high.

106. Owl, in typical 'twenties decorative style. France, early 1920s. Silver-plated bronze with glass eyes, 4 × $2\frac{1}{2}$ in (10 × 6 cm).

107. Centurion's head. U.K., *c.* 1928. Brass, $4\frac{3}{4} \times 3$ in (12 × 7.5 cm).

108. A dinosaur mascot advertised in 1926. U.K.

109. Head of an Indian chief. France, early 1920s. Nickel-plated soft metal, $5\frac{1}{2} \times 3\frac{1}{2}$ in (14 × 9 cm).

110. (*right*) Crouching figure of a naked man with a winged pilot's helmet and goggles, signed 'H.R.'. France, late 1920s. Soft metal, $4\frac{1}{2} \times 2\frac{1}{2}$ in (11.5 × 6 cm).

111. 'The Wind' signed 'Hansafray'. Germany, late 1920s. Chrome-plated soft metal, 4 × 5¼ in (10 × 13 cm).

112. 'The Pathfinder' designed by Regno. U.K., mid 1920s. Bronze, 3½ in (9 cm).

113. Icarus in flight. U.K., early 1920s. Silver-plated bronze, $4\frac{1}{4} \times 3\frac{3}{4}$ in (11 × 9.5 cm).

114. Flying batman, signed 'Sasportas'. France, mid 1920s. Silver-plated bronze, $4\frac{1}{4}$ in (11 cm).

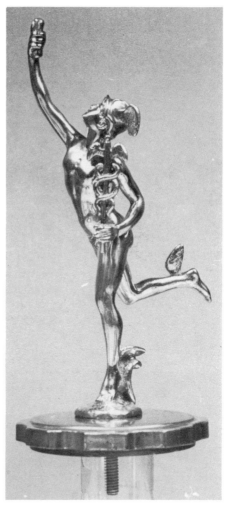

115. (*left*) This piper, Bulio, was probably inspired by a Roman bronze. U.K., mid 1920s. Chrome-plated bronze, 6½ in (16.5 cm).

116. (*below, left*) Young piping satyr, stamped 'Dit.Mar'. U.K., early 1920s. Silver-plated bronze, 2 in (5 cm).

117. (*below*) Mercury. U.K., *c.* 1910. Silver-plated bronze, 7 in (17.5 cm).

118. (*above*) Winged lady in flight, manufactured by A.E.L. U.K., early 1920s. Chrome-plated bronze, $4\frac{3}{4} \times 7\frac{1}{2}$ in (12 × 19 cm).

119. (*left*) 'Le point d'interrogation', a mascot commemorating the flight of Coste and Bellonte across the Atlantic. France, 1930s. Bronze, 5 in (13 cm).

120. (*below*) Mercury-Pegasus mascot produced by Rossi's engineering works in Eastbourne; priced at £12.12.0 this was one of the most expensive mascots. UK., 1932. Silver-plated bronze.

V. A man braced against the wind, made by F. Preiss, France, mid 1920s. Enamelled bronze, 6 in (15 cm).

IV. (*overleaf*) Peacock by René Lalique.
A clear glass version of this mascot
was produced earlier and is more common.
France, late 1920s. Glass, 7 in (18 cm).

121. Stylized
winged nymph on
a wheel, thrusting
forward a model
car, signed 'Darel'.
France, early
1920s. Silver-
plated bronze,
5½ in (14 cm).

122. Three Pegasus mascots: Left; Made by A.E.L. U.K., late 1920s. Chrome-plated bronze.
4¾ in (12 cm); centre: The Amilcar company mascot, stamped 'Darel'. France, mid 1920s.
Silver-plated bronze, 4 in (10 cm); right: Twin-winged Pegasus, made by A.E.L. U.K.,
mid 1930s. Chrome-plated brass, 4 in (10 cm).

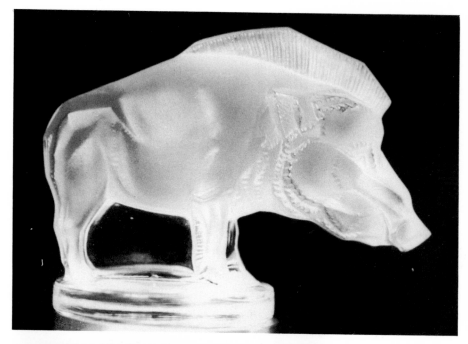

123. (*above*) 'Sanglier', signed 'R. Lalique'. France, late 1920s. Glass, $2\frac{3}{4} \times 3\frac{1}{2}$ in (7 × 9 cm).

124 (*left*) 'Tête de Coq', signed 'Lalique, France'. France, late 1920s. Glass, 7 in (18 cm).

125. 'Hirondelle', signed 'R. Lalique'. France, mid 1920s. Glass, $4\frac{1}{2}$ in (11 cm).

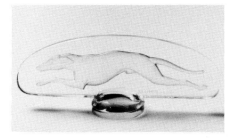

126. (*above, left*) An advertisement for Lalique mascots from a May 1929 issue of *Autocar*.

127. (*left*) 'Levrier', an etched medallion, signed 'R. Lalique France'. France, late 1920s. Glass, 6 in (15 cm).

128. (*top right*) St Christopher, an etched medallion, signed 'R. Lalique France'. France, mid 1920s. Glass, 4 in (10 cm).

129. (*bottom, right*) 'Tireur d'arc', an etched medallion, signed 'R. Lalique France'. France, mid 1920s. Glass, 4 in (10 cm).

130. (*opposite, above left*) 'Tête de Faucon', signed 'R. Lalique France'. France, mid 1920s. Glass, 2 in (5 cm).

131. (*opposite, above right*) Penguin, signed 'Etling, Paris'. France, early 1930s. Glass, $2\frac{1}{2} \times 5$ in (6.5 × 12.5 cm).

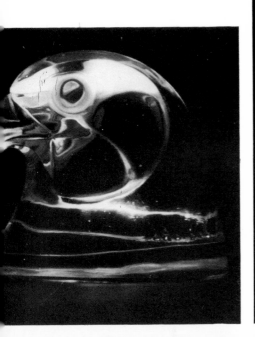

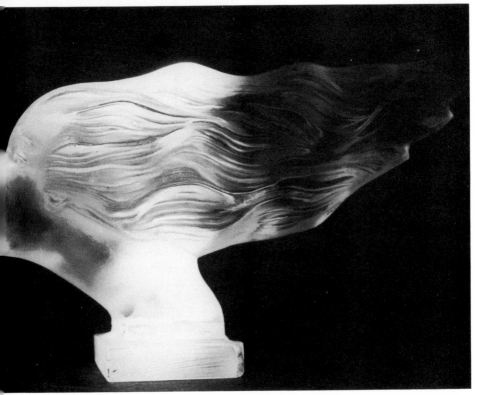

132. A Red Ashay illuminated mascot which is nearly an exact copy of Lalique's 'Victoire'. U.K., late 1920s. Glass, 3 in (7.5 cm).

# 4
# COMPANY MASCOTS

As a result of the spreading popularity of car mascots, many of the automobile manufacturers had decided by the late 1920s to establish the marque of their product by providing their own mascot either as standard equipment or as a recommended accessory. These were all intended to evoke speed, grace and elegance, and to be outstanding symbols sufficiently different from those of other manufacturers to be easily recognizable. Of course, many chose similar themes, and it is often extremely difficult to tell from which make of car a particular mascot comes, once it has been detached. Moreover many companies, particularly in the U.S.A. chose different mascots for the different models that they produced, and changed these from year to year. For example, the early Alvis had a hare, whereas later cars of that make were sold with an eagle; and in 1935 Packard produced two ranges of automobile and issued a pelican on the expensive model and the 'Goddess of Speed' on the less expensive one.

Some mascots issued by companies had their own names; Rolls Royce's 'Spirit of Ecstasy' is probably the most famous mascot of all, and one of the few still produced today. In France, where names for mascots were especially popular, Ballot called its symbol 'Renomée', Bec 'Vertige de la Vitesse',

Delahay 'Les Qualités de la Race' and Voisin its mechanical wings 'Cocotte'.

The easiest company mascots to recognize, and in many ways the least interesting, are those which consist simply of the first letter of the cars, name. Amongst the companies that sometimes used such 'initial mascots' are Austin, Bentley, Borgward, Daimler, Hupmobile, Morris, Studebaker and Talbot-Lago. Invariably these were streamlined with wings, comet tails or lightning streaks.

In the highly enjoyable automobile advertisements of the magazines of the period, the manufacturers practically never showed a mascot on their cars before 1930. At that point, the advertisements changed, especially in the U.S.A. The *Saturday Evening Post* of 1934, for instance, advertises the following cars with their mascots: Buick, Chrysler Airflow, Desoto Airflow, Dodge, Pontiac and Studebaker. In an issue of April 1934 the Auburn is shown without a mascot, but in one of the September issues of the same year the newly designed 1935 Auburn appears; the drawing of the car shows a disproportionately large mascot on its hood, emphasizing the change. In a November issue a sinister advertisement for Alemite lubrication shows a high speed collision between two cars, with the headline, 'Today 37 people will be killed or injured in tragic accidents resulting from faulty lubrication'. At the point of impact are a flying nymph on one car and a model aeroplane on the other.

In the following pages mascots provided by a number of different companies are described, with their origins and evolutions wherever this is possible. These are given in alphabetical order of the names of the manufacturing companies with the result that many of the more famous ones, such as the Rolls Royce mascot, appear towards the end. Well over four thousand makes of car have appeared since the invention of the automobile, of which many had mascots, and it is impossible to describe them all but it is hoped that this section will be of considerable use in identifying them.

**ALVIS** (*U.K., 1920–1967*)
This classic British car had many custom mascots mounted on its radiators by clients. In the 1920s the company provided its own mascot, a hare, which was

THE ALVIS FIREFLY.
A 12 H.P. 4-CYLINDER SPORTS CAR.

133. (*left*) An illustration showing the Alvis mascot, a firefly. U.K., 1932. Chrome-plated bronze.

134. (*above*) An Alvis mascot, a hare. U.K., 1926. Chrome-plated brass, $4\frac{1}{4}$ in (11 cm).

replaced by an eagle in the 1930s. On the 1932 Alvis Firefly a model of a firefly insect was installed.

**AMILCAR** (*France, 1921–1939*)
The car's name is an anagram of its financial backers, Messrs Lamy and Akar. A figure of Pegasus was used as the mascot from 1925; this symbol has

appeared at various times on many different makes of automobile, and it is sometimes difficult to recognize which were made by Amilcar, especially since their mascots changed in style over the years. Pegasus is an ideal mascot; the horse represents horsepower, while flight symbolizes speed. In 1926 Amilcar introduced a racing model, the C-6 Course, which, although it only had an 1100 cc engine, could reach 118 mph. Mascots were provided in three different sizes, large for the 8-cylinder model, medium for the 7CV, and small for the 5CV. In 1935, Amilcar produced a model called Pegasus, an example of a car being so closely identified with its mascot that the company gave it its name.

## ARMSTRONG-SIDDELEY
(*U.K., 1919–1960*)

The merger, in 1919, of the Armstrong-Whitworth and Siddeley-Deasy car companies gave birth to the first of the Armstrong-Siddeley cars; the company's intention was to produce a lower-cost, luxury car. At an early date a seated sphinx was chosen as the company's emblem and mascot because a journalist described the car as 'silent and inscrutable as the sphinx'. In 1931 this mascot was redesigned, the sphinx on the Thames embankment being used as its model. It became more and more stylized, especially after the war, until it finally evolved into a streamlined sphinx's head.

135. (*right*) The Sphinx on the London Embankment on which the Armstrong Siddeley mascot was modelled. U.K., 1878.

136. (*below*) The Armstrong Siddeley mascot, a sphinx. U.K., 1930s. Chrome-plated brass, $\frac{3}{4} \times 4$ in ($2 \times 10$ cm).

**AUBURN** (*U.S.A., 1900–1937*)
Several members of the Duesenberg company were called in to help the Auburn automobile company in 1934. The company's newly designed cars for that year met with resistance from a largely unenthusiastic public and had disastrously poor sales. Gordon Buehrig was hired to give the car a 'face lift' since little money could be spent on actual redesign at that stage. Although he created the famous boat-tailed super-charged 851 and 852 Speedsters and Phaetons for 1935, his immediate job involved improving the general appearance of existing models. He redesigned the fenders and radiator grille and added details learned at Duesenberg, including the use of a distinctive mascot; a winged lady, flying ahead of the car, was designed by part of his team.

Auburn was one of the first cars to have its radiator completely enclosed, with the cap inside and invisible. The mascot was fixed to the front end of the chrome strip that marked the hinge line along which the hood opened. On the

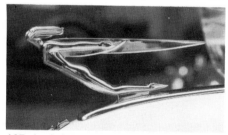

137. An Auburn mascot, a flying nymph, designed by Gordon Buehrig. U.S.A., 1935. Chrome-plated bronze, 4¼ in (11 cm).

1935 Speedsters, Buehrig added a detail he had originally used on the Duesenberg Speedster; a mascot was simply split in two and the halves were bolted on to the quarter panels just behind the doors on each side. The company was finally killed by the depression, which severely reduced the number of car companies in America.

**AUSTIN** (*U.K., started 1906*)
In its early years Austin, like other low price cars, did not provide a company mascot; however, Austin did produce moto-meters which often had decorative wings. As a result, wings were used as the company's emblem and some wing mascots appeared, although most Austin owners bought fantasy mascots from suppliers for their cars. In post-war years Austin introduced on some models a single wing, attached to the letter A as its company mascot.

**AUSTRO-DAIMLER**
(*Austria, 1899–1936*)
This elegant car was used by members of the court and high officials of the Austro-Hungarian Empire, who sometimes had mounted on it a double-headed eagle mascot. The company's mascot, a bow and arrow in a circle, was not unlike that of Mercedes-Benz.

138. The Austro-Daimler mascot. Austria, 1920s. Chrome-plated bronze, 5½ in (14 cm).

## BALLOT (*France, 1919–1932*)

This company had built marine engines before producing cars and adopted an anchor as its symbol. In the early 1920s it provided a complicated mascot called 'Renomée', meaning 'fame', which consisted of a nymph with windswept hair, standing on one leg beside a marine winch; she is shown holding a laurel crown in her left hand and announcing the car's fame through a trumpet held high in her right hand.

139. The Ballot mascot, 'La Renomée'. France, 1920s. Silver-plated bronze, 5½ in (14 cm).

## BECK (*France, 1920–1922*)

This short-lived French car provided a mascot called 'Vertige de la Vitesse', a figure of an apparently terrified girl holding her face in her hands and trying to keep her balance against an onrush of wind. There are several photographs of this mascot mounted on the radiator of a naked car chassis, showing how, in earlier days, companies sold cars which had to be sent to a coach builder.

140. (*right*) The Beck mascot, 'Vertige de la Vitesse', signed 'G. Poitrin'. France, 1920. Silver-plated bronze. 6¼ in (16 cm).

## BENTLEY (*U.K., started 1920*)

In 1929 Bentley Motors Ltd succumbed to the strain of the Great Depression and was bought by Rolls Royce. Soon afterwards it started supplying the famous 'Flying B' mascot which has been its mascot ever since. Early mascots had wings coming out from each side of the B; on later ones the wings sprout from behind the letter. Later the B evolved from leaning backwards to leaning forwards since it was necessary to move the wings further forward to allow the hood to open. A detail that is worth noting is that the Bentley mascot faces the right way from whichever side it is seen despite the fact that the letter B is not quite reversible. In fact the letter faces forwards when seen from the right of the car and backwards when seen from the left. This is achieved by giving the letter the shape of a sloping, squared eight, with a cleft taken out of the middle of the front on the right hand side and the middle of the back on the left hand side.

141. (*above*) The Bentley mascot, the 'Flying B'. U.K., late 1920s. Chrome-plated bronze, 3 × 8½ in (7.5 × 21.5 cm).

142-145. Designs for the mascot of the 1933 Derby Bentley which Charles Sykes, the creator of the Rolls Royce 'Spirit of Ecstasy', submitted to Rolls Royce. The single winged 'Flying B' was accepted and a few were produced. U.K. 1932-33.

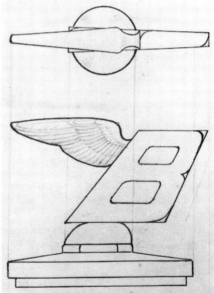

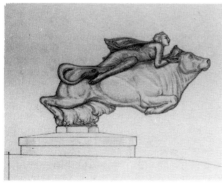

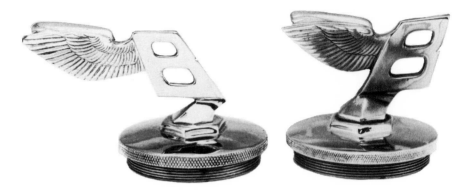

146. Two Bentley mascots. Left: U.K., 1930s. Chrome-plated bronze, $2\frac{3}{4} \times 3\frac{1}{4}$ in (7 × 8.5 cm). Right: U.K., 1940s. Chrome-plated bronze, $2\frac{3}{4} \times 3$ in (7 × 7.5 cm).

This mascot has survived virtually unchanged. However, unlike those of Bentley's sister car, the Rolls Royce or of its rival, the Mercedes, Bentley mascots since the 1960s have been attached directly to the top of the radiator grille, without a base in the form of a false radiator cap.

### BERLIET (*France, 1935–1939*)
Berliet, which produced cars until World War II but has only built trucks since then, introduced the patriotic symbol of a Gaulois warrior's head on the 1929 6-cylinder models. This highly stylized sculpture was clearly influenced by Voisin's 'Cocotte'.

### BIANCHI (*Italy, 1899–1939*)
This Milan-based company built medium priced, rather conservative cars in the 1920s and 1930s. Unusually for an Italian manufacturer, a company mascot, the Visconti Eagle, was supplied with the chassis. This heraldic bird was the emblem of the Visconti, Dukes of Milan throughout the Middle Ages, and of their successors, the Sforzas.

### BORGWARD (*Germany, 1939–1961*)
In the early 1950s Borgward used a streamlined B on some of its models. This

mascot is sufficiently dissimilar from that of the Bentley to be easily distinguishable.

### BRASIER (*France, 1906–1930*)
In the patriotic fervour prevalent in all countries in 1914, Brasier installed an armless veiled figure of Victory as its mascot.

### BUCCIALI (*France, 1923–1933*)
Some very unconventional automobile designs, far ahead of their time, appeared in France in the 1920s. The Bucciali, perhaps the most extraordinary French car ever built, incorporated features that did not become common until the 1960s. The most exotic Bucciali, the famous double 8, appeared in 1931; this 16-cylinder front-wheel drive car was powered by two 3.8-litre, 8-cylinder engines which filled the entire length of the car's enormously elongated hood. The whole car was very low and the cockpit small, giving it a remarkable silhouette. The extremely distinctive Bucciali mascot closely paralleled the sleek lines of the car. It is a chrome-plated figure of a stork, placed almost horizontally on an elongated rectangular base. A large silhouette of this bird was repeated in chrome on either side of the hood.

**BUCHET** (*France, 1911–1929*)
This company used Pegasus as its mascot; unlike Amilcar's Pegasus, the design was very baroque.

**BUGATTI** (*Germany, and subsequently France, 1909–1956*)
Ettore Bugatti, one of the great automobile geniuses, was responsible for designing and constructing the most famous of sports cars. None of these had mascots on their distinctive horse-shoe-shaped radiators. However, when he introduced the Type 41 model, probably better known as the Bugatti 'Royale', a 12.7-litre, 8-cylinder-engined car with an enormous chassis, he installed a massive mascot of an elephant standing on its hind legs, its trunk raised. The sculpture for this was designed by his brother, Rembrandt Bugatti, who was famous in his day as a sculptor and was especially well known for his animal figures. The elephant stands on its hind legs, and was intended to show how even such an enormously heavy beast could be light-footed, as was the car. Bugatti's timing was poor; although it was originally planned that there should be twenty-five of these cars, only six were built between 1932 and 1933; on five of these the mascot was fixed. Only three of the cars were sold.

147. The Buick mascot, a goddess's head. U.S.A., mid 1920s. Soft metal, 4¼ in (11 cm).

**BUICK** (*U.S.A., started 1903*)
When mascots became fashionable in the United States in the late 1920s, Buick, like most other cars built by General Motors, produced its own mascot—a goddess' head. In 1927, a forward leaning, streamlined figure of a goddess very much in the style of the period, was introduced. When Buick resumed building cars after World War II it installed as its mascot, until 1954, an elongated dart within a chrome circle.

148. A Buick mascot, a goddess. U.S.A., 1934. Chrome-plated brass, 7 in (18 cm).

**CADILLAC** (*U.S.A., started 1903*)
America's most prestigious car, the Cadillac, is named after Sieur Antoine de la Mothe Cadillac, a French soldier and adventurer, who explored the New World, and finally became Louis XIV's Governor of Louisiana. In 1701 he founded Detroit, the town that became the capital of the automobile industry in the U.S.A. The company's emblem is the coat of arms of La Mothe Cadillac on a shield, crowned by a nine-pointed coronet.

Early Cadillacs were sometimes sold with moto-meters, which had the name of the car or the company's coat of arms engraved on them. When mascots became popular in the 'twenties Cadillac owners began to put custom or fantasy

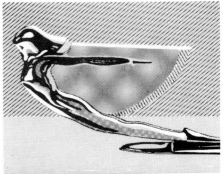

149. The Cadillac mascot; this goddess was mounted on the V-8 and V-12 models. U.S.A., 1934. Chrome-plated brass, 8 in (20 cm).

150. A Cadillac goddess with transparent plastic wings which was mounted on the 8 and 12 cylinder models. U.S.A., 1936. Chrome-plated brass and plastic.

mascots on their cars until finally the company introduced its own as an approved accessory. Of these one of the first was made in Canada, probably around 1929. It shows a herald with the Cadillac emblem on his livery, blowing a trumpet from which hangs a flag bearing the name Cadillac. The first actual company mascot, introduced in 1930, was a graceful figure of a heron, its neck outstretched and its wings pointing upwards; this was discontinued in 1934 since it was considered too close in design to Hispano-Suiza's stork and Packard's pelican. In its place was put the figure of a goddess leaning forward against the wind, her hands stretched back, with a long scarf flying behind her—an exquisite statuette very much in the Art Deco style. This mascot was standard on V8 and V12 engined cars, while the V16 used a goddess ornament which was heavier, with pronounced wings, more closely resembling a forward-leaning version of Rolls Royce's 'Spirit of Ecstasy'. Unlike Rolls Royce however, Cadillac's goddess changed from year to year, and is thus less well known. In 1936 on the V8 and V12, she was made more streamlined and stylized, and was given transparent plastic wings. In 1937 her hair was longer and more

deeply etched, as were her plastic wings. She continued to become more streamlined with narrower plastic wings, thus mirroring the increased streamlining of the car. The heavier V16 goddess was slightly altered in 1938 to match the design of the car and was used until 1940, the last year that the V16 model was built. In 1941 Cadillac introduced a new all-metal goddess, which was stretched and lengthened in 1942; both of these mascots had a practical purpose. They served as the handle and release for the hood-latching mechanism, and so can be recognized by a break two-thirds down the goddess's body. After World War II Cadillac switched to a highly stylized sculpture of the goddess, by now more like a twin-winged dart with a human face. This was continued until 1956; in that year on the Eldorado model it was replaced by small twin fins at the centre of the hood while other Cadillacs retained the goddess.

The fin, perhaps the most influential styling element introduced in the U.S.A. after World War II, has an interesting origin. First planned for Chevrolet, it was considered so daring that General Motors decided to introduce it initially on Cadillacs, their most expensive and standard-setting car. Conceived by

Harley Earl, it was first used for the tail lights on 1948 models. It was adopted, as a patriotic gesture, from the twin-tailed Cadillac-powered Lockheed P38 Lightning fighter of World War II and is an example of the influence of aero-engineering on automobile design. Like Renault's tank, it is also an example of a patriotic, military symbol being used on a car. The tail fin was much copied all over the world throughout the 'fifties and 'sixties, and in many ways is the best symbol of the post-war American dream. In 1957 and 1958 Cadillac retained independent twin fins mounted on the centre of the hood as a mascot. In 1959 these were displaced to the side of the car, above the headlights.

In the 1970s, when a revival of the more traditional type of mascot began in the U.S.A., the Cadillac coat of arms surrounded by a wreath was re-intro-duced as standard equipment on the 1972 Eldorado and has been obtainable as a company manufactured optional accessory on all Cadillacs ever since. Because of safety regulations it is quite small, spring-mounted and made of a lightweight alloy and plastic. Cadillac has also re-introduced the V16 goddess as an optional extra although its use is illegal in some states.

## CASE (*U.S.A., 1909–1927*)
Another good example of a patriotic mas-cot was that of Case, a large American eagle with its wings spread, standing on a globe.

## CHENARD-WALCKER
(*France, 1901–1946*)
Once again the symbol of the eagle was used as a mascot, in this case the Napoleonic eagle of France which symbolized the Empire, courage and military strength. Borne at the head of Napoleon's regiments to emulate the Roman legions, the eagle also stands for victory; in 1923 Chenard-Walcker's 3-litre machines finished first and second in the first 24-hour Le Mans race ever held, and also won the 1924 *Circuit de Routes Paveés*.

## CHEVROLET (*U.S.A., started 1911*)
Since the beginning of motoring in the United States, Chevrolet has rivalled Ford in the field of best-selling, inex-pensive cars. A number of mascots have appeared at various times on the Chevrolet since the company introduced them in the 1930s; a flying bird, patented in 1933, was one commonly used. It is worth noting that Chevrolet did not put the radiator cap inside the hood of its cars until several years after this had be-

151. Cadillac goddess, mounted on the V-16 model. U.S.A., 1940. Chrome-plated brass, 8¾ in (22 cm).

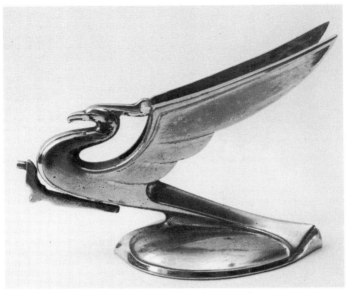

152. Chevrolet mascot, a bird. U.S.A., 1933. Chrome-plated brass, $7\frac{1}{2}$ in (19 cm).

come common practice on more expensive cars.

### CHRYSLER (*U.S.A., started 1923*)

Chrysler cars have had several mascots. Hermes's winged hat was introduced in 1924 and plain wings were used on some models from 1925 until the early 1930s when a leaping antelope, fixed by its hind legs to the radiator, was installed.

The famous, though unsuccessful, airflow model with its totally aerodynamic design (in fact, the first such car ever to appear) was introduced in 1934. Chrysler advertised the car as being 'Balanced like an arrow in flight', and it was suggested that potential customers should 'Try the magic carpet of 1934'. The mascot on this car was a streamlined airfoil of Chrysler's traditional two wings, swooping back along the hood. This motif was repeated in profile on the rear-wheel spats of the car, and is the precursor of the streamlined emblems that were typical of American design twenty years later.

On the early Chrysler Imperial and the three parade Phaetons built in 1952, the mascot was a free standing eagle with outspread wings.

153. The Chrysler Airflow hood ornament. U.S.A., 1935. Chrome-plated brass, 3 in (7.5 cm).

VI. (*above*) Five prancing horses in silhouette, 'Cinq Chevaux', signed R. Lalique, France, mid 1920s. Glass, 4 in (10 cm).

VII. (*below*) 'Tête de Bélier', signed 'R. Lalique, France', late 1920s. Glass, 6 in (15 cm).

VIII. Hispano-Suiza mascot, a stork. France, 1918. Silver-plated bronze, 8¼ in (21 cm).

154. The Citroen
mascot, a swan.
France, early
1930s. Chrome-
plated soft metal,
4 in (10 cm).

155. 1913 Clement;
the lizard mascot
can be seen on the
bonnet. France.

156. The Clement
mascot, a lizard.
France, 1913.
Brass, lifesize.

## CITROEN (*France, started 1919*)

Citroen installed a stylized figure of a swan on its 1924 5CV model. This symbolized grace and was also supposed to suggest the 'free floating' engine that the company introduced.

## CLEMENT (*France, 1909–1922*)

The cock, a symbol of France, was installed on the radiator caps of this car in 1915 and 1916, and again for the short period that this company existed after World War I. In earlier years a lizard had been mounted on the hood itself.

**CONTINENTAL** (*U.S.A., 1933–1934*)
Continental were one of the first companies to build the engines for cars and trucks and by 1933 were producing them for one hundred makes of car and over half the trucks in America. DeVaux used Continental engines and when it went bankrupt, Continental decided to recoup some of the money owed to them by using the DeVaux factory to produce three cars in different price categories, each cheaper than competing makes; they introduced the Ace Big Six and the Flyer, both 6-cylinder models, and the Beacon, a 4-cylinder one. The company mascot was a figure of a woman with outstretched arms and a plume-like headdress, mounted on a base on which was inscribed the name of the model. The whole project was a failure and the company stopped producing cars although the mascot continued to be sold at just under a dollar.

**CROSLEY** (*U.S.A., 1939–1952*)
Powell Crosley, who had pioneered the manufacture of radios, refrigerators and electrical appliances, developed this 'minicar', which competed quite successfully against full-size cars in the United States, where it was virtually unique; the only comparable car being the Bantam, an American version of the baby Austin Seven.

Although very small, many models were produced including sedans, four-seater convertibles, station wagons, vans and open two-seater sports cars.

Until production was halted by the war effort in 1942, Crosleys could be bought in department stores as well as through car dealers! Priced at $325 it was the least expensive car in the U.S.A., undercutting the Bantam by more than $60. However it shared one feature with the most expensive American car, the Cadillac: a hood ornament which

also served as a latch handle for opening the bonnet. Crosley's mascot had the company's name embossed on either side and had to be twisted for the hood to open.

**DAIMLER** (*U.K., started 1896*)
The only company mascot seen on Daimlers is the letter D with a comet's tail. However, coach-built Daimlers often had custom mascots installed. As the favourite car of England's royal family, the British lion frequently appears on royal Daimlers, and photographs of the cars of the royal fleet lined up outside Windsor or Buckingham Palace in the 1930s all show massive lions standing or seated on radiator caps. Royal mascots were frequently transferred from one Daimler to its successor when the cars were changed.

**DELAHAYE** (*France, 1894–1954*)
This pioneering French company had already built six hundred cars before the end of the last century. Although Delahaye took fourth and fifth place in the Paris–Marseilles–Paris race of 1896, the company showed little interest in racing in this century until 1935 when it took over the Delage company. It introduced the Type 135 in 1936 which took the second, third, fourth and fifth places in the French sports car Grand Prix and won the Monte Carlo rallies of 1937 and 1939, as well as the 1938 24-hour race at Le Mans and the 1939 'Fastest Sports Car Race' at Brooklands. The type 145 introduced in 1937 could reach 165 mph. Plain wings were used as mascots from 1925 to 1930 when the rather pompous 'Les Qualités de la Race' was introduced. This mascot was obviously influenced by Gabriel Voisin's effort to produce a car mascot that epitomized industrial design. After World War II Delahaye had a difficult time

157. A Delahaye advertisement in which their mascot features prominently.

since the luxury sports car market had atrophied. It sold 483 cars in 1950, and although it won the 1951 Monte Carlo rally for the second and last time, it only sold forty-four cars that year.

**DESOTO** (*U.S.A., 1928–1960*)
Desoto first introduced their mascot in 1928. This was the figure of a warrior who, as years went by, became streamlined to the point of abstraction, lying

on the front of the car. On the Airflow model, introduced in 1934, an abstract airfoil similar to that on the Airflow Chrysler, was used. As on the more expensive car, this motif was repeated on the rear-wheel spats.

### D.F.P. (*France, 1906–1926*)

This company, named after its builders, Messrs Doriot, Flandrin and Parent, never fully recovered from World War I, particularly since its British distributor, W. O. Bentley, decided after the war to build his own cars. It is one of the several companies that chose, as its mascot, the greyhound to epitomize speed and grace.

### DODGE (*U.S.A., started 1914*)

On some of their early cars the Dodge brothers mounted their company emblem in a lozenge on the radiator cap. This consisted of the initials, D.B. in enamel in a six pointed star superim-posed on the globe, and was supposed to symbolize world-wide acceptance of their cars. In the 1930s a prancing ram was introduced as their mascot, which, as cars became more streamlined, evolved from being a free-standing figure into an elongated wedge, with only the ram's head and horns retained.

### DUESENBERG (*U.S.A., 1920–1937*)

The most prestigious car produced in American in the late 'twenties and 'thirties was unarguably the Duesenberg. At the age of twenty-five, Gordon Buehrig had been hired as Duesenberg's designer, and, for them, he created the most beautiful cars of the period, such as the Derham Tourister. This automobile, which had a long, model J chassis, was painted green and yellow and had a huge running girl as a mascot. When Gary Cooper walked into the 1930 salon in Los Angeles and saw it, he bought it on the spot.

158. Three Dodge mascots, streamlined Rams' heads. U.S.A., Chrome-plated brass. Top: 1953. 5 in (12.5 cm). Centre: 1946. 6 in (15 cm). Bottom: 1942. 10 in (25 cm).

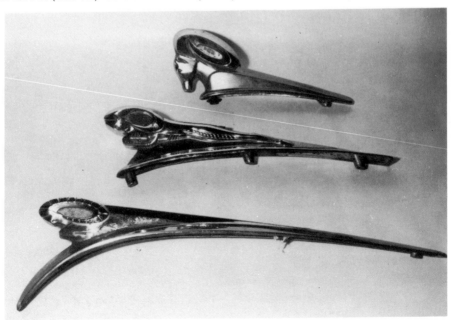

Buehrig also designed the company mascot and has explained how and why this happened. When Duesenbergs were first built, the company felt that the make should be so distinctive that a nameplate and radiator ornament would be superfluous. However, owners apparently wearied of telling curious questioners what the make was and several asked that a nameplate be added; many also wanted mascots and bought them in all shapes and sizes. The company felt that most of these mascots looked terrible on Duesenbergs and that all were out of character, so it was decided to add a nameplate and to design a hood ornament that would enhance the appearance of the car and add to its distinction. As Buehrig points out, the company's economic situation had a bearing on the design. Unlike larger companies which produced a large number of cars, Duesenberg built less than a hundred a year. Therefore, whereas other companies were prepared to invest in tooling so as to economize on labour, Duesenberg could better afford high labour costs than additional tooling. So the mascot was designed to be made in the company shop without any special tools from two flat sheets of brass. These were cut to profile with a few lines etched into either side of the upper piece on a milling machine; a hole was drilled in the base piece and the two were then brazed together and chrome plated. This highly stylized bird, which echoed the eagle on the company's nameplate, was then mounted on to the radiator cap, where it certainly enhanced the car's beautiful lines.

## EDSEL (*U.S.A., 1957–1959*)

The Edsel is probably the best-known failure of the automobile industry. Introduced in 1957 during the recession, it failed completely to capture the public's imagination, notwithstanding an extensive advertising campaign. Ironically, it has, in recent years, become a collector's item, being regarded as the epitome of the American multi-coloured and chromium-plated bad taste of that period. It is amusing to think that Ford, which produced the splendid Lincoln Continental Mark II only a short while before, could also design the Edsel, especially since both were proclaimed as traditionalist revivals. The Edsel had a much publicized vertical grille, harking back to pre-war cars, and of course it also had a mascot. This was a coat of arms, set in a circle and fixed above the radiator; along with the Continental it is the precursor of the hood ornament revival in the United States which began fifteen years later.

## ESSEX (*U.S.A., 1918–1932*)

The Essex was introduced as a low-priced car by Hudson in 1918, and increased Hudson's sales in the U.S.A. enormously. It was also a success as an export, being particularly popular in England. The Essex mascot is a winged man.

159. The Essex mascot. U.S.A., 1920s. Chrome-plated soft metal, $4\frac{1}{4}$ in (11 cm).

**FARMAN** (*France, 1920–1931*)
This French company was originally an aeroplane-engineering firm and, like Voisin, the luxury cars they built were clearly influenced by their experience with aircraft. They produced a 6.6-litre car in 1920, and in 1927 a 7.5-litre car which had an aluminium block and crank case. The company only made a total of 120 cars, and failed at the beginning of the depression. It intro-

160. The Farman mascot, Icarus. Stamped 'G. Colin Fondeur Unis'. France, 1920s. Silver-plated bronze, 6 in (15 cm).

duced in 1922 as a mascot a large figure of Icarus called 'La Conquête de L'Air'; this was a reproduction of a sculpture by Colin George which commemorated the first winged flight of Santos-Dumont. Despite its weight, this mascot was mounted on the light racing cars the company entered in competitions.

Lindbergh should own a 1928 26 hp sedan. Although the company linked the car's successful air-cooled engine to advances in aviation, it nonetheless was so influenced by the appearance of contemporary automobiles that in 1925 the car was redesigned with a totally unnecessary fake radiator which was crowned by a large mascot of a rampant lion. This so vexed the car's original designer that he resigned from the company.

### GARDNER (*U.S.A., 1919–1931*)
This American company is known for its low-slung, front-wheel-drive cars. The company's mascot was a flying griffin.

161. (*above, left*) The Graf und Stift mascot. Austria, 1920s. Silver-plated bronze, 6 in (15 cm).

162. (*left*) The Gardner mascot, a griffin. U.S.A., mid 1920s. Chrome-plated brass.

163. (*below*) The Guy mascot, an Indian chief's head. U.K., early 1920s. Aluminium, 4¾ in (12 cm).

### FORD (*U.S.A., started 1903*)
Through the years Ford have produced many different mascots. The classic V8 Ford Phaeton of 1935 had the well-known Lincoln greyhound as its mascot. The early post-World War II Fords were sold with the helmeted head of a warrior, while in 1957, like Edsel, Ford revived a small, traditional mascot.

### FRANKLIN (*U.S.A., 1901–1939*)
Franklin was the only company in the U.S.A. to produce air-cooled engines throughout its entire existence. A Franklin car broke the San Francisco–New York record in 1904, and when air-cooled engines became common in aeroplanes Franklin made the most of this in its publicity. The 1928 and 1929 3.9-litre models were called 'Airman' and it arranged that Colonel Charles

## GRAF UND STIFT
(*Austria, 1907–1938*)
This company is perhaps most famous for historical reasons as it produced the car in which the Archduke Franz Ferdinand was assassinated at Sarajevo in 1914; the actual car, a 1912 Graf und Stift, is on display in Vienna's Heeresge-schichtliches Museum. The company provided a large lion as a mascot, the biggest being on the 1921 8-litre SR1 model. A smaller version, following the trend towards smaller mascots as cars became more streamlined, was mounted on the 1936 5.9-litre SP-8.

## GREGOIRE (*France, 1903–1924*)
Probably the largest mascot ever produced was the archer made by this early French automobile company. It weighed approximately one and a half kilos or three and a third pounds.

## GUY (*U.K., 1919–1925*)
Guy built luxury cars and was the first company in England, after Vulcan, to introduce a V8 engine, an idea imported

164. The Hillman Melody Minx mascot. U.K., 1934. Chrome-plated brass, $4\frac{1}{4}$ in (11 cm).

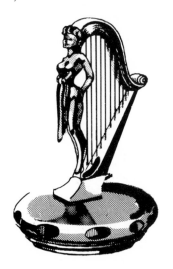

from the U.S.A. Perhaps because of this, an American Indian chief's head was used as the mascot; the company motto, 'Feathers in our Cap', was engraved on the headdress. After 1925 the company ceased building cars but continued to produce commercial vehicles.

## HILLMAN (*U.K., started 1907*)
Hillman created their most distinctive mascot for the Melody Minx. Introduced in 1934, the Melody Minx was the first British car to have a radio as standard equipment and this was reflected not only in the car's name, but also in its mascot, which was a miniature harp in the form of a nymph. The idea behind the mascot probably came from the enormously successful Busby Berkeley musical comedy, 'Fashions of 1934'. A sequence in this film, 'The Hall of Human Harps', prompted a now famous article by an outraged mother entitled, 'I don't want my daughter growing up to be a human harp'.

## HISPANO-SUIZA
(*France and Spain, 1904–1944*)
This Spanish company used Swiss technology to build cars in both Spain and France, the most famous being built at the French works. The company mascot, a flying stork, is probably the best known after Rolls Royce's. It was adopted by the company in honour of George Guynemer, the enormously popular French World War I aviator. It was the emblem of his flying squadron, with which he won fifty-four aerial combats before being shot down in 1917. The bird's body is free standing, its legs trailing behind, and the mascot is fixed to the radiator cap by the tips of the wings. This was the first winged mascot to use this type of mounting, although many copies and imitations have since been made. Hispano-Suizas were also built during the mid-'twenties

165. George Guynemer's aircraft, on which is painted the stork which became Hispano-Suiza's emblem.

under licence by Skoda in Czecho-slovakia. Photographs of these some-times show a winged arrow mounted as a mascot. This is still Skoda's emblem today.

## HORCH (*Germany, 1900–1939*)

This well-known German car became part of the Automobile Union group in 1932. Later Horches are sometimes seen in World War II movies as German staff cars. The company mascot was two wings, sometimes mounted on a globe, and sometimes parted by an arrow.

## HOTCHKISS (*France, 1903–1955*)

Hotchkiss was a company of munitions manufacturers and had once provided Napoleon III's ordinance. It began to build cars in 1903, and its emblem consisted of two crossed canons with a shell between them. There is a photo-graph of a Hotchkiss with a model canon mounted as a mascot.

## HUDSON (*U.S.A., 1909–1957*)

Hudson used several company mascots. In 1932, when they replaced the Essex, their lower-cost car, with the Terraplane, they used different radiator grilles and mascots to distinguish between the Terraplane and their other car the Hud-son, which looked very much the same.

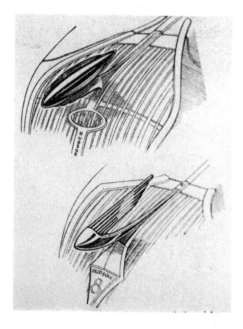

166. The Hudson company used differently designed radiators and mascots to distinguish their otherwise identical cars, the Hudson and the Terraplane. Top: Hudson. U.S.A., 1930s. Chrome-plated brass. Bottom: Terraplane. U.S.A., 1932-1937. Chrome-plated brass.

**HUMBER** (*U.K., 1898–1974*)

This company in the Rootes group produced many different expensive cars, some of them with mascots. The most noteworthy mascot appeared in the 1930s after the safety-conscious Sir William Rootes had ordered the production of an updated snipe mascot for the Snipe model. This had its jutting, pointed beak made of red rubber, and the whole mascot was spring-mounted. Fantasy mascot manufacturers produced a copy with independently moving wings.

the first Jaguar mascot appeared. However William Lyons was unimpressed by this original design and commissioned the sculptor Gordon Crosby, to produce a better one. This was a great success and was used until the 1960s when it first shrank in size and finally vanished completely, a victim of safety regulations and economics.

**LA LICORNE** (*France, 1901–1950*)

True to its name, this company adopted the unicorn as its mascot.

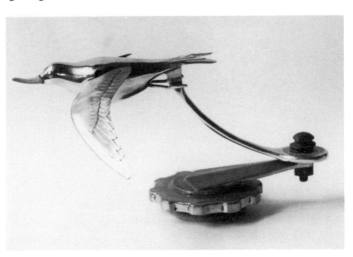

167. A fantasy mascot produced for the Humber Super Snipe which had a rubber beak and wings which flapped. U.K., c. 1930. Chromium-plated metal and rubber, 5½ in (14 cm).

**HUPMOBILE** (*U.S.A., 1908–1940*)

The letter H, mounted in a circle, was introduced by this company as its mascot in 1932. The mascot was remarkable only for its size and consequently did not last long.

**ISIS** (*Czechoslovakia, 1923–1925*)

This short-lived company designed a low-bodied, light car. Drawings show a mascot in the form of the Egyptian goddess; however, only prototypes of the car were ever built.

**JAGUAR** (*U.K., started 1945*)

The Swallow company started producing the S.S. Jaguar in 1936, and in 1937

**LASALLE** (*U.S.A., 1927–1940*)

The Lasalle was launched in 1927 to fill the price-gap between the Cadillac and the Buick. It was entirely designed by General Motors' chief stylist, Harley Earl, and although less expensive and smaller, was manufactured to Cadillac standards. Like its more ostentatious sister, it was named after a French explorer, this time René Robert Cavalier Sieur de la Salle, who had claimed all Louisiana for Louis XIV in 1682. In 1928 General Motors introduced, as the Lasalle mascot, a small figure of the explorer holding a sheet of paper in his left hand and a hat in his right. In 1929, a winged man was provided which, in

168. (*right*) The SS Jaguar mascot by Desmo. U.K., 1937. Chrome-plated brass, 8 in (20 cm).

169. (*below*) A Lasalle mascot. U.S.A., 1929. Chrome-plated bronze, $4\frac{1}{4}$ in (11 cm).

170. Two Lincoln greyhounds; the one in the rear was also fitted on the V8 Ford Zephyr. U.S.A., early 1930s. Chrome-plated brass, $9\frac{1}{2}$ in (24 cm).

1934, was replaced by a mascot completely abstract in design which became, over the years, more streamlined to reflect the lines of the car. In its final years, Lasalle introduced a rather clumsy, rocket-like ornament, and although a more graceful one was planned for the 1941 model, it was never built.

## LINCOLN (*U.S.A., started 1920*)

This, the most prestigious car built by Ford, offered as a mascot an elaborate, engraved sculpture of a greyhound in the late 1920s. When the greyhound was introduced on the Ford Phaeton in 1935, Lincoln substituted a stylized comet on its Zephyr models. This mascot was also used on the Continental from 1940 until the U.S.A. entered the Second World War.

## LINCOLN CONTINENTAL
(*U.S.A., 1955–1957, restarted 1968*)

In early 1952 the Ford Motor Company's top management decided to build a prestige car specifically to wrest away from General Motors Cadillac's reputation as the best American car. The remarkable Continental Mark II, which appeared in late 1955, was similar, in the distinction of its design, to its namesake, the Lincoln Continental which ceased being produced in 1948; it was also very European in its simplicity and fine proportions, quite different from the increasingly chromed and finned idiom exemplified by its direct competitor, the Cadillac Eldorado. As part of the subdued ornamental

171. The Lincoln Continental mascot. U.S.A., 1954. Chrome-plated brass.

trim on the Continental a discreet hood mascot was included; its simple design was directly influenced by such traditional marks of quality as the Mercedes star, and in sharp contrast to the large, stylized, chrome rockets and jet shapes affixed to the nose of most contemporary American cars. When the Mark II was discontinued after two years because it cost so much more to build than the company could sell it for, the mascot was retained on the new line of Continentals.

This first American post-war resurrection of a traditional car mascot is still retained today and has certainly influenced others. In the 1970s many American cars have begun to sprout small distinctive mascots of this type, and, as with the Duesenberg and Auburn Speedsters, the mascot occasionally appears on other parts of the car as well. It is either fixed to the side panels, or the roof pillars (now usually covered in fake hide), or even etched in glass in the small rear 'vanity windows' that have appeared in expensive American automobiles today. Because of safety considerations, these mascots are now spring-mounted and made of plastic or alloys.

The 1955 Continental mascot was really an afterthought. There had not even been a decision on whether it was to have one until the directors of Ford asked to be shown what the design team had in mind at a board meeting the next day! Robert Thomas made a quick sketch and his design was approved unanimously. This was slightly refined and it was then handed over to the company's engineering group. It presented some problems since, as with many of the new Continental's components, the standards demanded were beyond manufacturers' capabilities. Another team member, Harley Copp, remembered an article on a unique method used to manufacture sights for anti-aircraft guns. This was investigated and the problem was solved, although at a cost per mascot in excess of that of a complete grille of a contemporary Ford!

## LORRAINE-DIETRICH
(*France, 1897–1934*)
Cars built by Lorraine-Dietrich won both the 1925 and 1926 Le Mans 24-hour race. Like so many other companies, it provided a statuette of a greyhound as its mascot.

## MARMON (*U.S.A., 1902–1930*)
Marmon was one of the well-known American companies that vanished with the depression; the company's mascot was a bronze eagle mounted on a scrolled base.

## MATHIS (*Germany and subsequently France, 1898–1950*)
The Strasbourg-based Mathis company, like Bugatti, changed its nationality with the return of Alsace-Lorraine to France in 1918. It was well known for its light 'Emy' models (the founder's first name was Emile), which were promoted with advertisements extolling the car's fuel economy. The company's mascot was a small sculpture of a swept-back flame.

## MAYBACH (*Germany, 1921–1941*)
Maybach produced the aero-engines which powered Count Zeppelin's famous air-ships. The company's first car was entered in the 1921 Berlin motor show and from 1930 to 1939, the well-known Maybach-Zeppelin car, which had a 12-cylinder engine, was built. This car, in the 1930s, shared with the Mercedes-Benz 770 the reputation of being Germany's most exclusive car. The car's finish and construction were of the highest quality and also the engine extremely quiet. The

Maybach mascot was a chrome outline of a shield surrounding the company's emblem.

## MERCEDES-BENZ
*(Germany, started 1926)*
In 1901 Daimler Motoren Gesellschaft, one of the first automobile producers, designed and built a high performance modern car for Emil Jellinek, an Austrian business man and diplomat, who raced under the pseudonym 'Herr Mercedes', from his daughter's first name, which became attached to the car he drove. In 1925 German Daimler merged with another automobile company, Carl Benz and the resulting company, Daimler-Benz AG, have built Mercedes-Benz cars ever since.

The three-pointed star had been part of the Daimler family emblem and was adopted by the Daimler company in 1909. The Benz emblem was a laurel wreath; and the new company emblem was the star encircled by a laurel wreath; soon after the merger, mascots appeared showing the encircled star. On Mercedes sports cars built after World War II, the mascot slipped down to become the chrome centrepiece of the much widened grille. On other Mercedes cars, the mascot has remained. It is worth noting that of all today's cars with mascots, the most famous, Mercedes, Rolls Royce, and Bentley, have all retained a traditional radiator grille integrated into the contemporary design of their bodies, and two of them, Rolls Royce and Mercedes, have the mascot mounted on a fake radiator cap base. This is clearly one reason why mascots on these cars do not seem out of place. For the last few years these mascots have been spring-mounted for safety and as a precaution against the vandalism provoked by the presence of such luxury automobiles in the street.

172. The Mercedes-Benz mascot. Germany, from 1925. Chrome-plated bronze and, in later models, stainless steel, 4 in (10 cm).

## MESSIER *(France, 1926–1931)*
This unsuccessful French company is famous for having introduced pneumatic suspension in lieu of conventional springs. The Messier suspension system is the basis of that used in Citroens since the 1960s. The company's mascot was a stylized eagle perched on a globe designed by Brau, which should not be confused with the more realistic eagle and globe mascot of Case.

## MINERVA *(Belgium, 1899–1939)*
The famous car company produced its first car in 1900 and continued until World War II, and was known as 'La Marque Doyenne' of Belgium. The company mascot was a head of the Roman goddess Minerva, the patron of the arts and industry. It was created by Pierre de Soete, one of whose designs took first prize in the 1921 *Salon de l'Automobile* mascot competition in Paris.

**MORRIS** (*U.K., started 1913*)
The Morris Oxford was built at Cowley near Oxford in 1912; the Cowley model was introduced in 1919. The company's emblem shows an ox crossing a ford, the coat of arms of the City of Oxford. Although a modestly priced car, it was nonetheless seen from time to time in the 'twenties and 'thirties with a figure of an ox mounted as a mascot. In later models of the post-war Morris Minor,

173. A Packard mascot. U.S.A., 1940s. Chrome-plated brass, 9 in (23 cm).

a comet-like mascot, with the letter M in silver on a red enamelled lozenge, was mounted. This was the last of the inexpensive company mascots to be produced and served a dual purpose because, as well as being decorative, it was a handle with which to lift the hood.

**NASH** (*U.S.A., 1917–1957*)
Nash cars sported many different mascots during the company's existence; of these the most memorable were those used on the Lafayette model of 1936 and on the Farina-designed Nashes of the 'fifties; the former had the letter L in a comet-shaped lozenge, the latter a streamlined nymph which looked very much like a woman lying on her stomach sunbathing, with her chin resting on her hands.

**PACKARD** (*U.S.A., 1899–1958*)
The Packard brothers built their first car in 1899, and formed their company, the Packard Motor Car Company, in 1903. Their emblem was the coat of arms of the Packer family of Baddlow in Essex which had been brought from England to America in the seventeenth century by one by their ancestors, Samuel Packard. Above the family crest was 'A pelican in her piety' plucking her breast to feed her young. This long-necked bird was used as one of the two Packard mascots offered by the company when it introduced them as standard accessories in the early 1930s. In 1932 the company offered a lower priced car, the 120 (subsequently called the Eight), which had a different mascot, the winged figure of a woman holding an automobile wheel in her outstretched arms called the 'Goddess of Speed'. This is similar to the 'Spirit of Triumph', a popular French mascot designed by Bazin in 1920 and often fitted on to export models of the Italian Isotta-Fraschini car. The pelican was revived when production was resumed after World War II, the last ones being mounted on the 1952 and 1953 models. The mascot of 1952 had high raised wings, and looked somewhat out of place, a true, old-fashioned radiator mascot on the hood of a later wide-grilled modern car; as a concession to the times, the 1953 pelican had his wings clipped and flattened. From 1954 until the company's sad demise, stylized

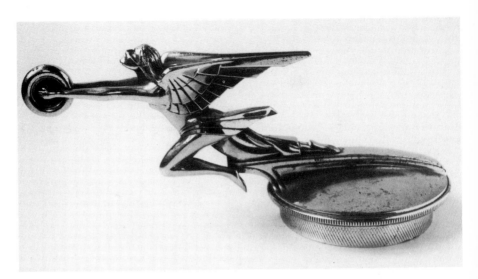

174. The Packard 'Goddess of Speed'. U.S.A., 1930s. Chrome-plated brass, 10 in (25 cm).

175. Left: The Peugeot 'Lion de Belfort', signed 'M. Marx'. France, available from 1922. Silver-plated bronze, 5½ in (15 cm). Right: A Peugeot lion, signed 'Boulanger'. France, 1922. Bronze, 3½ in (9 cm).

IX. Kneeling girl. France, mid 1920s. Green-patinated bronze, $3\frac{1}{4}$ in (8 cm).

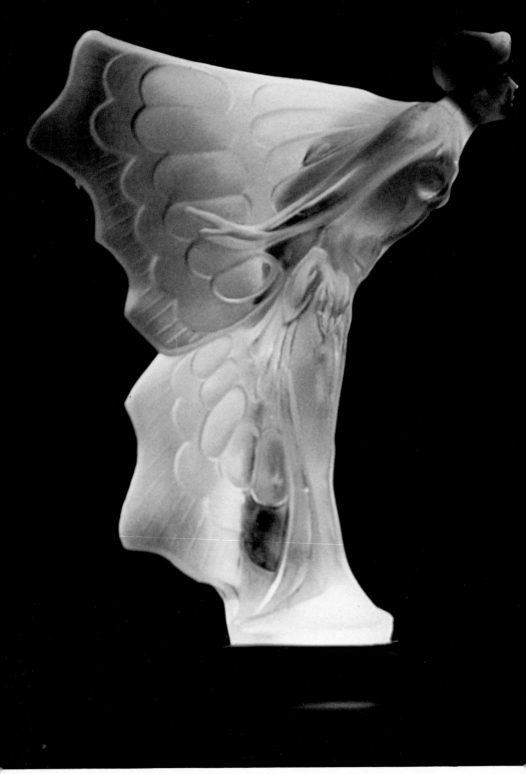

X. 'Butterfly girl' made by Red Ashay. U.K., late 1920s. Glass, 8½ in (21.5 cm).

rockets typical of contemporary designs replaced the family bird.

## PEUGEOT (*France, started 1889*)

The Peugeot factory was in Belfort. The Prussians had been defeated outside the city in 1871, and to commemorate this, a statue of a lion was made by Bartholdi, who also designed the Statue of Liberty in New York. The lion became Peugeot's emblem and one of their earliest cars was called the Lion-Peugeot. As early as 1922 the company magazine, 'Peugeot Revue', advertised a lion mascot. This was a standard accessory until the 1960s when the 403 model went into production. The largest lion mascot was on the 18 CV car, but it became smaller and more streamlined until 1938 when just the open mouthed head alone was mounted. A good ex-

kneeling archer named 'Tireur d'Arc'. The car was also distinguished for having its headlamps incorporated into the wings as early as 1913. The archer evolved slightly over the years, becoming heavier, shedding his clothes and settling into a more comfortable position.

176. The Pierce Arrow mascot. Archer. U.S.A., late 1920s. Chrome- plated bronze, 4 in (10 cm).

177. A Peugeot lion. France, late 1930s. Silver-plated bronze, 13 in (33 cm).

ample of the lion's head mascot can be seen on the 402 model of 1938, which like the Airflow Chrysler, carried a profile of its mascots on its rear-wheel spats.

## PIERCE ARROW (*U.S.A., 1901–1938*)

This American luxury car originally provided as a mascot a model of a car wheel on which was mounted an arrow bearing the name 'Pierce'. The later and better known mascot was a small statue of a

## PLYMOUTH (*U.S.A., started 1928*)

The Chrysler corporation introduced a 4-cylinder, inexpensive car in 1928. It was called Plymouth after the home town of America's Pilgrim Fathers. A *Saturday Evening Post* advertisement in June 1934 asks the potential buyer, 'Wouldn't you gladly pay $5.00 more to get the safest car and the most comfortable?' It illustrates the point, showing the front end of a new Plymouth priced at $630.00 with a '$5.00 more' tag attached to the mascot. As a mascot, logically enough, a model of the May-flower was chosen. On early models the ship was free standing, while in the late 'thirties it became a silhouette within a tear-drop shape. As the car became more streamlined, a very stylized design recalling the ship's sails evolved.

**PONTIAC** (*U.S.A., started 1926*)
General Motors began building Pontiac cars in 1926. The car's name derives from Pontiac, the home town of the original company bought by General Motors in 1909. This town had been named after the great Ottawa Indian chief, who united the North American Indian tribes in rebellion against the British in 1763. In 1934 a 6-cylinder model was intro-duced.

The mascot has always represented an Indian chief; on early models a figure of a running Indian leaning forwards was used but soon the Indian chiefs head alone became the standard mascot. In the late 'thirties and 'forties, Pontiac, like Cadillac, began to use plastic in all its mascots; the silhouette of the headdress was made of this sometimes transparent, sometimes amber coloured material; the profile of the face was also occasionally made of plastic. As mascots became more streamlined, especially in the 1950s, Pontiac installed a com-promise between the traditional Indian and the new jet-plane type of mascot; a pair of wide wings coming out from behind the Pontiac's chief's head.

**RENAULT** (*France, started 1898*)
Renault played an important role in the French military effort during World War I. Its 1100 cc 2-cylinder Parisian

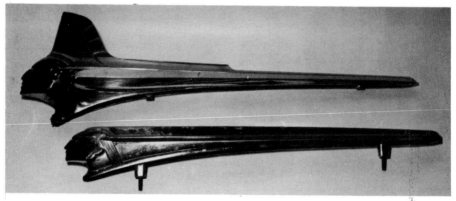

178. (*above*) Two Pontiac mascots, highly stylized Indian Chief's heads. U.S.A., chrome-plated bronze. Top: 19 in (49 cm); Bottom: 17 in (43 cm).

179. (*left*) The Pontiac mascot, an Indian chief's head. U.S.A., late 1920s. Chrome-plated bronze with bronze face, 4 in (10 cm).

taxis became famous when the entire fleet was commandeered to rush French soldiers to the Marne where they stopped the German advance. Also the caterpillar tank, built for the French army, contributed significantly to the final victory. To commemorate this, Renault installed a model tank on its radiator caps in 1918. It should be noted that the radiators on Renaults at that time were still mounted behind the engine, so the mascot is just ahead of the windshield.

## REO (*U.S.A., 1904–1936*)
A large American eagle was provided by the company on its 1909 16 hp model; later models had a torso of Mercury with winged hat and outstretched left arm, fixed at the waist to the radiator cap.

## ROCKNE (*U.S.A., 1932–1933*)
The short-lived Rockne was named after Knute Rockne, the legendary Norwegian-born chemist who became the football coach for Notre Dame University in South Bend, Indiana, the home town

181. The Pontiac chief's head incorporated into jet plane. U.S.A., 1955. Chrome-plated metal and plastic, 6 in (15 cm).

of the Studebaker. The brain-child of two indigent car engineers, Vail and Cole, the Rockne was built by Studebaker as an inexpensive model to compete with Ford and Chevrolet. The car mascot was the letter R mounted inside a wheel, with a single swept-back wing.

## RÖHR (*Germany, 1929–1935*)
This company, like so many others, installed the first letter of its name on the radiator caps of its cars.

## ROLLAND-PILAIN
(*France, 1906–1931*)
The Rolland-Pilain was fairly popular for a brief period after World War I. In 1929 it built a Franco-American luxury car on a large chassis with an American Continental engine, but the elegant coachwork was somewhat marred by the use of artillery wheels. A winged sphinx was the company's mascot.

## ROLLS ROYCE (*U.K., started 1904*)
Rolls Royce has the most famous car mascot, the 'Spirit of Ecstasy', which was designed in 1911 by Charles Sykes, an eminent artist and sculptor of the day. At that time the most popular

180. The Rolland-Pilain mascot, a winged sphinx. France, 1924. Chrome-plated bronze, $8\frac{1}{2}$ in (21.5 cm).

mascot was the comic cop which marred the elegance of Rolls Royces. So, at the suggestion of the second Lord Montagu of Beaulieu, Sykes designed the 'Spirit of Ecstasy', a girl who, in the artist's own words, 'has selected road travel as her supreme delight and has alighted on the prow of a Rolls Royce car to travel in the freshness of the air and the musical sound of her fluttering draperies'. Although this figure was based on the various models who sat for Sykes, the features were unmistakably those of Eleanor Thornton, Lord Montagu's secretary. So are those seen on another figure, designed by Sykes, which was not selected by Rolls Royce, but was later adopted by Lord Montagu for his personal car.

Eleanor Thornton was not destined to survive her immortalization in the 'Spirit of Ecstasy' for long. In the winter of 1915 Lord Montagu, then

183. The Rolls Royce 'Kneeling Lady', designed by Charles Sykes, was mounted on Phantom III. U.K., 1929. Chrome-plated bronze, 3¾ in (9.5 cm).

182. A Rolls Royce 'Spirit of Ecstasy'. This small version was mounted on the Silver Cloud and the Silver Shadow and subsequent models. U.K., 1955. Steel, 3½ in (9 cm).

Inspector of Mechanical Transport in India, returned to his post with his secretary, sailing on the S.S. *Persia*. On December 30th the liner was torpedoed off Crete and it sank in a few moments. Lord Montagu was blown to the surface by an underwater explosion, but his secretary was never seen again.

The 1913 catalogue depicted only two cars equipped with the 'Spirit of Ecstasy' and no mention of it is made in the list of approved accessories. However Rolls Royce were sufficiently pleased with the acclaim granted to the 'Spirit of Ecstasy' to enter her into the 1920 Paris '*Concours des Bouchons des Radiateurs* where she was awarded the gold medal. The next year she was officially mentioned as factory equipment, included in the price of each complete car.

Until then Sykes personally put the finishing touches to each mascot before it was affixed to a car, and each early Rolls Royce mascot was slightly different, since different wax moulds were used.

184. The Rolls Royce 'Spirit of Ecstasy', designed by Charles Sykes, was mounted on the Phantom I and the Phantom II. U.K., 1911. Chrome-plated bronze, 7 in (17·5 cm).

Early Rolls Royce radiators were made of polished bronze and the mascot was finished accordingly. Later the radiator shell was made of nickel, and the mascot was nickel-plated; still later, when stainless steel was used for the radiator shell, the mascot was chromium-plated. As cars became lower and radiators relatively higher, a tall upstanding mascot seven inches high looked a little incongruous and also impaired the driver's view of the road, so a 'Kneeling Lady' version of the mascot evolved and was introduced in the mid-1930s. This mascot

was used on the Phantom III and on the 25/30 hp and Wraith cars until World War II, and on post-war Rolls Royces, until the introduction of the Silver Cloud in 1955, when it was replaced by a smaller version, three and a half inches high, of the original standing lady.

After the war the company obtained mascot castings from various sources, but in 1957/8 a foundry was built at Crewe and the company has since then made its own mascots. The metal used is one of the 'Nimonics', an untarnishable steel which requires no electroplating, and when polished closely resembles stainless steel.

It is worth noting that like Mercedes, but unlike its sister car the Bentley, Rolls Royce still mounts its mascots on a small base shaped like a radiator cap; water is no longer added from outside and the cap will not unscrew, yet the original mounting has always been retained.

In recent years Rolls Royces have been sold to the United States, the Middle East and other foreign markets, often in vivid colours and with such recent fashions as Vinyl tops. As part of this trend away from traditional restraint, many Rolls Royce mascots have been supplied in a gold colour.

### ROVER (*U.K., started 1904*)

The emblem of the Rover company is a Viking ship under full sail, with the figure-head of a roving Viking's head wearing a winged helmet. Various models of this head, as well as standing Vikings have been provided by the company as mascots.

185. (*left*) A Rover mascot, a Viking. U.K., 1930s. Chrome-plated bronze, $4\frac{1}{4}$ in (11 cm).

**SIZAIRE** (*France, and subsequently Belgium, 1923–1931*)
The two Sizaire brothers, Maurice and Georges built cars in France until 1929 and subsequently in Belgium. The company's mascot was an angular flying wedge, inspired by the custom mascot designed for them by the futurist sculptors, Jan and Joel Martel.

**SIZAIRE-BERWICK**
(*England and France, 1913–1927*)
Before World War I this company built a car with a radiator which was a copy of Rolls-Royce's. It was subsequently sued and had to modify its design; in addition to making it pointed, an eagle was added as a mascot.

186. A Rover mascot, a Viking's head. U.K., 1930s. Chrome-plated bronze, 3¾ in (9.5 cm).

187. The Sizaire Six mascot. France, 1928. Chrome-plated bronze.

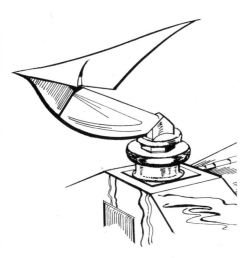

188. The Star mascot. U.K., 1922. Chrome-plated bronze, 5½ in (14 cm).

**STAR** (*U.K., 1898–1932*)
This comparatively little-known company introduced as its mascot in 1922 a six-pointed star, in the centre of which was a representation in relief of a nymph.

189. The Studebaker mascot, a circumscribed swan. U.S.A., mid 1930s. Chrome-plated metal.

## STUDEBAKER (*U.S.A., 1902–1966*)

Studebaker introduced a streamlined swan emblem as their first company mascot in the mid-1930s. This was sometimes surrounded by a chrome oval ring. A traditional Mercedes type mascot, the letter S enclosed in a ring of chrome, was revived in 1961 on the Hawk model.

## STUTZ (*U.S.A., 1911–1935*)

Stutz cars were the delight of rich sportsmen in the United States in the roaring 'twenties. The Bearcat Speedsters of 1914–1925 were marvellous sports cars and, before the company introduced their own mascot, were frequently mounted with custom-made models of cats. In the late 1920s an Egyptian emblem, the winged head of Ra, the sun god, was used as a mascot. The Black Hawk, a 4.9-litre speedster, was introduced in 1927 and took second place in the 1928 24-hour Le Mans race. This model sometimes sported a sundial on its radiator cap, a continuation of the sun-god theme. The

company eventually failed in 1935, a victim of the depression.

## TALBOT (*U.K., 1903–1938*)

This famous pre-war English company produced many models, some of which had the letter T as a hood-ornament.

190. The Stutz mascot, 'Ra', the sun god. U.S.A., early 1920s. Chrome-plated metal, $3\frac{1}{4}$ in (8.5 cm).

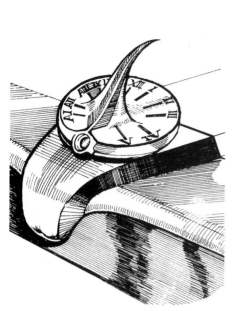

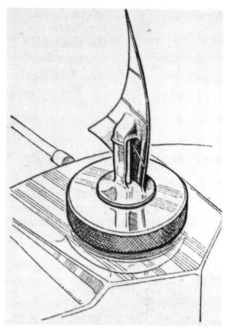

191. The Stutz Black Hawk mascot, a
sundial. U.S.A., 1929.

192. A Talbot mascot containing a thermometer. U.K., 1929. Chrome-plated brass.

193. The Talbot-Lago initial mascot. France, 1951. Chrome-plated brass, 2 × 4 in
(5 × 10 cm).

194. The Triumph Dolomite mascot, a nymph. U.K., 1936. Chrome-plated bronze, 8 in (20 cm).

Another mascot provided by the company on later models was a sail which incorporated a thermometer.

**TALBOT-LAGO** (*France, 1945–1959*)
The Darracq company, which had built well-known Grand Touring and Grand Prix cars before the war, attempted, with the Talbot-Lago, to resurrect such glorious machines. The initials, TL, were mounted on some models with a comet's tail; others had just the letter T in a chrome circle.

**TRIUMPH** (*U.K., started 1923*)
The Triumph company emblem showed an enamelled globe with the oceans marked in blue, the land masses in plain chrome except the British Empire which was in red; later on all land was marked in red. A nymph standing on the globe was provided as a mascot with the Dolomites introduced by Triumph in 1936.

**TROJAN** (*U.K., 1922–1926*)
This car, built by Leyland Motors, was named Trojan to suggest strength and steadfastness. The car mascot was a Trojan warrior's helmeted head.

**TURCAT-MERY** (*France, 1898–1928*)
This French car won the 1922 Monte Carlo rally, the first ever held. Built in Marseilles, it adopted as its mascot the regional insect, the cicada, one of the few cases of an insect used for this purpose. In addition to an elegant V-shaped radiator, the Turcat-Méry had such refinements as a bell to warn against falling oil pressure.

**UNIC** (*France, 1905–1939*)
In the 'twenties and 'thirties Unic built handsome touring cars and provided them with the figure of a centaur, carrying a bow and some arrows, as a mascot.

195. The Trojan mascot. U.K., 1930. Aluminium alloy, 4½ in (11.5 cm).

Since 1939 the company has built only trucks and continues to do so today in association with Fiat, but the emblem has been retained.

**VAUXHALL** (*U.K., started 1903*)
The first Vauxhall car was built in 1901 by the Vauxhall Ironworks at Lambeth. The name Vauxhall derives from Fulk le Breant, a nobleman at the time of King John, whose house at Lambeth was known as Fulk's Hall. Fulk's emblem was the griffin, a heraldic beast, half lion, half eagle, which was adopted in 1927 as the car's mascot. The griffin sometimes held a standard with the initial 'V' engraved on it.

**VOISIN** (*France, 1919–1939*)
Gabriel Voisin, the World War I aircraft engineer, produced cars which had rev-

196. (*above*) The Unic mascot, a Centaur, signed 'F. Bazin' and inscribed 'Unic'. France, mid 1920s. Soft metal, $5\frac{1}{2}$ in (14 cm).

197. (*right*) The Vauxhall mascot, a griffin, stamped 'Joseph Fray Ltd'. U.K., 1927. Silver-plated bronze, $3\frac{1}{2}$ in (9 cm).

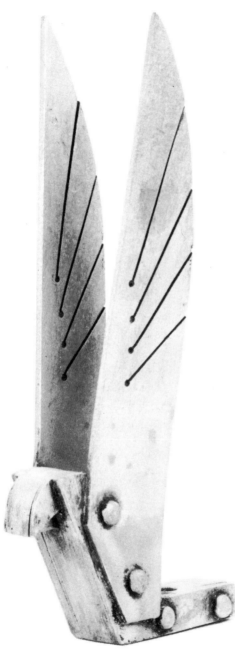

198. The Voisin mascot, 'Cocotte'. France, 1920s and 1930s. Aluminium, 9 in (23 cm).

olutionary aluminium-bodies and which were always remarkable for unorthodox looks as well as their excellent performance. In 1920 he designed the famous 'Cocotte' or 'Chick', that became the immediately recognizable symbol of his cars. The aircraft company's emblem had been an Egyptian winged scarab, and 'Cocotte' evolved from it as a 'tongue in cheek' response to the rather pompously decorative mascots being produced at the time. Although it began as a joke it was enormously influential. In a letter Voisin explains how this happened:

'One day I was discussing the radiator ornaments that were rather tentatively beginning to appear. We had made a few somewhat unhappy attempts ourselves; rabbits, fish, elephants, small "works of art" and so on had appeared in succession on our radiator caps without much success, when a friend of mine, Marcel Lejeune, the painter, gave his opinion on the subject. "A radiator mascot must be a mechanical ornament. Thus if you machine-cut the shapes you want out of sheet metal and assemble these with visible rivets you are bound to get a satisfying form." I immediately designed the "Cocotte". I had the piece made up and that same day I fixed on the hood of my car the two aluminium wings which are now so well known to the public. This little joke did not particularly satisfy me, in fact it had not really pleased any of us, but within a couple of days three clients had demanded one and, notwithstanding my protests, I was forced to produce them. A week later we built fifty of them. In 1928 we produced five thousand and despite my efforts the "Cocotte" remains standing on our radiator caps. Then taxis began to copy our chick which naturally we had patented. We had to go to court, which we did successfully, to stop "Cocotte" from becoming the brunt of worse jokes. Up until then our firm was the only one inflicted with this piece of ill luck, but its spreading became inevitable when I saw the Delahaye company bring out its insignia "Les Qualités de la Race", in 1930. The bad taste that we had unleashed has today made the rounds of all radiators in all shapes.'

## VULCAN (*U.K., 1902–1928*)

As this company's name suggests, Vulcan, the god of industry, was provided as a mascot.

## WOLSELEY (*U.K., 1899–1974*)

Wolseley installed the letter W with a streaming tail as a mascot on several models in the 1930s and 1940s. On Hornet models a stylized version of the insect was used.

## 'REPLICARS'

Since World War II collecting antique cars has become an established hobby. However, many of the more sought after machines have become prohibitively expensive; also their parts are impossible to come by and old cars are difficult to insure, so a number of replicas of old-time favourites have appeared. These include copies of the SS Jaguar, the model A Ford, the M.G.TD., the pre-war Alfa Romeo, the pre-war B.M.W., the SSK Mercedes, and the three most famous American classics, the Cord, the Duesenberg and the Auburn. Even the owners of real Duesenbergs and Auburns have bought replicas for every day use. Although a Duesenberg copy sells for over $25,000, this is cheap in comparison to the real thing. A few years ago a model J Duesenberg, in good condition, one of less than five hundred built between 1929 and 1935, was sold for $207,000. Replicas of the Auburn and the Duesenberg are perfect copies and include the Flying Lady mascot. The Excalibur, not an exact copy of the SSK

Mercedes but a specialized car based on it, comes with an imitation of the Mercedes mascot, the sword 'Excalibur' mounted within a chrome circle. Imitations of parts of old cars are sometimes added to modern ones, often with absurd results, for instance, fake Ford or Rolls Royce grilles are sometimes installed at the front of rear-engine Volkswagens; mounted on these one may see mascots, often travesties of the original.

199. The Vulcan mascot, the god Vulcan. U.K., 1915. Brass, 4¾ in (12 cm).

# 5
# MASCOTS AFTER WORLD WAR II

After World War II, cars in the U.S.A. and most other countries were more streamlined, the wheel guards were no longer independent but fully integrated into the car body and radiator caps had been put beneath the hood. As a result radiator grilles were lower and wider and so no longer suitable as bases for large, high standing mascots. Also, the inventiveness of the first years was no longer evident and, with the impact of the Second World War on the automobile industry in general, mascots disappeared almost entirely. In Europe only Rolls Royce, Bentley and Mercedes have continued to install mascots on their cars and even then on the Mercedes sports car, the three-pointed star was moved down to become part of the design of the radiator grille. On other cars, such as B.M.W. and Alfa Romeo, which before the war had distinctive grilles, the old design was incorporated in miniature as the central motif of the new grille.

However there developed in the United States a new style of mascots frequently modelled on jet planes, which more suited the new streamlined cars. While these mascots sometimes had highly abstracted human or animal features, they were part of the increasingly chromed and aerodynamic decor rather than a separate and distinctive emblem. The traditional type of mascot was reintroduced by Ford in their Lincoln Continental of 1955; two years later the unsuccessful Edsel was equipped with an adaptation of the old type of mascot as was the Studebaker Hawk in 1961. These three were the precursors of today's revival.

For some years mascots had been produced with some functional justification, for instance illuminated glass mascots, such as those made by Lalique, were supposed to serve as parking lights; other mascots were designed to deflect

200. Bird in Flight. This mascot was designed to deflect insects from the car's windscreen. Chrome-plated tin, bakelite, with glass eyes, 5½ in (14 cm).

201. Abstract airfoil, signed 'Sabino'. France, mid 1920s. Glass, $4\frac{1}{4}$ in (10.5 cm).

202. This running hare is still in production. U.K., early 1920s. Silver-plated bronze, $5\frac{1}{2} \times 3$ in (14 × 7.5 cm).

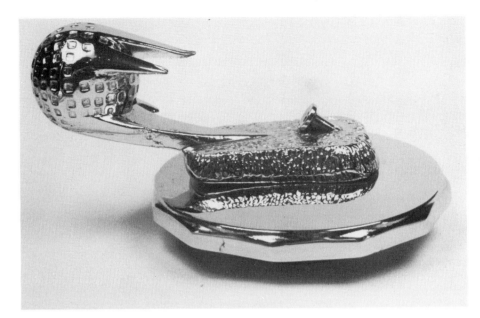

203. 'Golf Ball in Flight'; another version of this mascot was made in enamel, with the golf ball in white, the grass in green and the tee in white. U.K., 1935. Chrome-plated bronze, 4 in (10 cm).

204. A very large bullterrier mascot. U.K., early 1930s. $5\frac{3}{4} \times 8$ in (14.5 × 20 cm).

insects from car windscreens. More significant than this vague uneasiness about the purpose of mascots was the fear that mascots might impale pedestrians, or that in an accident these missile-shaped objects might literally fly off and cause additional damage. It was in fact stringent safety regulations that finally did away with heavy car mascots. So when nostalgia for the days when motoring had been a sport, and for the 'twenties and 'thirties generally, brought about a revival of interest in mascots and they were reintroduced by all the major American car companies, they had to be small, spring-mounted and made of some lightweight alloy or plastic. Since the mid-1960s, however, it had not been unusual to see mascots of the bulldog, horse and jockey and golfer variety. These are mounted somewhat inappropriately on the wide, flat hoods of modern American cars, most frequently station-wagons inside which can be seen the golf clubs or tennis racquets of the country club set.

Not all countries have the same concern for the safety of pedestrians. In Greece, Turkey, and Middle and Far Eastern countries buses and trucks frequently sport large, inferior copies of

famous mascots, such as the Lincoln greyhound, the Jaguar mascot, the prancing gazelle and many of the nymphs common in Europe and America in previous decades.

## COLLECTING

Car mascots have appeared in several exhibitions of twentieth-century art. At the Musée des Arts Décoratifs in Paris, the *Les Années 25* exhibition of 1966 and the exhibition held in 1976 to commemorate the fiftieth anniversary of the great exhibition of 1925 both showed some Lalique mascots and the Futurist ones designed by Joel and Jan Martel. In Minneapolis in 1971 the 'World of Art Deco' exhibition included the Martel mascots, a silver plated bronze rabbit made by Becquerel in 1925, a silver-plated bronze sphinx with an ivory face

206. A newspaper boy, his paper is inscribed 'The London cry—Taxi'. U.K., early 1920s. Chrome-plated bronze, 3 in (7.5 cm).

205. Prancing gazelle, designed for the Singer Gazelle. U.K., late 1930s. Chrome-plated brass.

207. Two pages from a 1928 issue of *Autocar* which contain an article on mascots.

7. H. Jenks, Ltd., 54, Ebury
Street, Pimlico, S.W.1 .. 30s.
8. A. E. Lejeune, Ltd., 132,
Great Portland Street, W.1 £3 3s.
9. W. G. Coram, 140, Victoria
Street, Bristol .. .. 10s. 6d.
10. North London Carrying Co.,
Carlton House, Regent
Street, S.W.1 .. .. £10 10s.
11. A. E. Lejeune, Ltd., 132,
Great Portland Street, W.1 £2 2s.
12. North London Carrying Co.,
Carlton House, Regent
Street, S.W.1 .. .. 50s.
13. Dunhills, Ltd., 359, Euston
Road, N.W.1 .. .. 55s.
14. Etienne et Cie, 75-7, Paul
Street, Finsbury, E.C.2 .. 30s.
15. North London Carrying Co.,
Carlton House, Regent
Street, S.W.1 .. .. 52s. 6d.
16. Arthur Knowles, John Harper
Street, Willenhall .. .. 12s. 6d.

Ltd., actually markets a greyhound
ridden by a monkey—a very topical
touch. The same firm also offers
mascots representing most of the
sports, such as tennis, Rugby football, and so on.

Notable for fine detail work is the
range offered by the North London
Carrying Co., who, in addition to
many other styles, specialise in animals and birds painted in
natural colours. One model
stands out far above the rest.
It is an eagle, measuring some
14in. from wing-tip to wing-
tip, and exquisitely finished.
It is, of course, only suitable
for the largest cars.

Rather different is the wide
range of London Motor Accessories, made up of various
insects and reptiles. These are intended to be fastened to the front of
the radiator. At the opposite end of
the scale in respect of subject is Dunhills, Ltd.'s, attractive study of a
woman playing a mandolin.

Perhaps the most interesting of the
assortment of Desmo, Ltd., is the
figure of a python, with head up-
raised in anger, while S. Smith and
Sons (M. A.), Ltd., have some attractive birds and animal heads. H.
Jenks, Ltd., have a wide selection.

Among other models Etienne et
Cie. offer the inevitable greyhound,
as well as a very shiny seal.

### MASCOTS.

1. Desmo, Ltd., 31, Stafford
Street, Birmingham .. 27s. 6d.
2. Arthur Knowles, John Harper
Street, Willenhall .. 11s. 6d.
3. S. Smith & Sons (M.A.), Ltd.,
Cricklewood, N.W.2 .. £3 15s.
4. Desmo, Ltd., 31, Stafford
Street, Birmingham .. 17s. 6d.
5. H. Jenks, Ltd., 54, Ebury
Street, Pimlico, S.W.1 .. 27s. 6d.
6. S. Smith & Sons (M.A.), Ltd.,
Cricklewood, N.W.2 .. £3 15s.

*The latest idea in mascots made of
Lalique glass.*

17. Etienne et Cie, 75-7, Paul
Street, Finsbury, E.C.2 .. 42s
18. Etienne et Cie, 75-7, Paul
Street, Finsbury, E.C.2 .. 7s. 6d.
19. North London Carrying Co.,
Carlton House, Regent
Street, S.W.1 .. .. 42s.
20. North London Carrying Co.,
Carlton House, Regent
Street, S.W.1 .. .. £3 17s. 6d.
21. North London Carrying Co.,
Carlton House, Regent
Street, S.W.1 .. .. £2 12s. 6d.
22. London Motor Accessories,
40, Leicester Square, W.C.2 29s. 6d.
23. S. Smith & Sons (M.A.), Ltd.,
Cricklewood, N.W.2 .. £4

24. C. Haseler & Son, Ltd., 94,
Bridge Street West, Bir-
mingham .. .. 10s. 6d.
25. North London Carrying Co.,
Carlton House, Regent
Street, S.W.1 .. .. 37s. 6d.
26. Pride & Clarke, 158, Stock-
well Road, S.W.9 .. .. 6s. 6d.
27. Desmo, Ltd., 31, Stafford
Street, Birmingham .. 17s. 6d.
28. Dunhills, Ltd., 359, Euston
Road, N.W.1 .. .. 30s.
29. Etienne et Cie, 75-7,
Paul Street, Fins-
bury, E.C.2 .. 42s.
30. Desmo, Ltd., 31,
Stafford Street, Bir-
mingham .. .. 35s.
31. Dunhills, Ltd., 359,
Euston Road,
N.W.1 .. .. 50s.
32. S. Smith & Sons
(M.A.), Ltd.,
Cricklewood, N.W.2 £7
33. A. E. Lejeune, Ltd.,
132, Great Portland
Street, W.1 .. £2 15s.
34. Desmo, Ltd., 31, Stafford
Street, Birmingham .. 27s. 6d.
35. Pride & Clarke, 158, Stock-
well Road, S.W.9 .. .. 7s. 6d.
36. Desmo, Ltd., 31, Stafford
Street, Birmingham .. 24s. 6d.
37. A. E. Lejeune, Ltd., 132,
Great Portland Street, W.1 £2 2s.
38. Etienne et Cie, 75-7, Paul
Street, Finsbury, E.C.2 .. 37s. 6d.
39. A. E. Lejeune, Ltd., 132,
Great Portland Street, W.1 £3 3s.
40. Etienne et Cie, 75-7, Paul
Street, Finsbury, E.C.2 .. 10s. 6d.
41. H. Jenks, Ltd., 54, Ebury
Street, Pimlico, S.W.1 .. £2 2s.
42. North London Carrying Co.,
Carlton House, Regent
Street, S.W.1 .. .. 55s.
43. S. Smith & Sons (M.A.), Ltd.,
Cricklewood, N.W.2 .. £2 2s.
44. Dunhills, Ltd., 359, Euston
Road, N.W.1 .. .. 30s.
45. Breves, Ltd., Imperial Court,
2, Basil Street, S.W.3,
Lalique Glass .. .. 63s. each.

### RADIATOR ORNAMENTS.

1, 2, 3, 4, 6, 7 and 8. London
Motor Accessories, 40,
Leicester Square, W.C.2 .. 30s. each.
5. W. G. Coram, 140, Victoria
Street, Bristol .. .. 25s.

REPRESENTATIVE RADIATOR ORNAMENTS

1      2      3      4      5      6      7      8

208. Another page from the 1928 issue of *Autocar* giving a key to the mascots
illustrated in plate 207.

209. (*left*) Four
'Futurist' mascots
by the twin
brothers, Jan and
Joel Martel. They
were made for
Robert Mallet
Stevens, Le
Courbusier, Gabriel
Voisin and the
Sizaire brothers.
France, 1920s.
Silver-plated
bronze, each
approximately 8 in
(20 cm).

210. (*below*)
'Telcote Pup'. U.K.,
early 1920s.
Chrome-plated
brass, 5 in (13 cm).

by R. Sertorio and Lalique's eagle's
head.

Car mascots have become collectors'
items. Most collectors fall into two
distinct categories; motoring enthusiasts who collect mascots as souvenirs of
the splendours of early motoring, and
collectors of twentieth-century decorative art, for whom mascots provide
examples of all the fashions and artistic
trends of the 'twenties and 'thirties.
There are others, such as collectors of

model aeroplanes or of military memorabilia, who are specifically interested in patriotic or humorous mascots from war periods. Generally, the most sought after are custom mascots, well-known early Company mascots, and glass fantasy mascots.

Mascots can be found in antique shops, flea markets, secondhand stores, and junk shops, and also in sales of works of art. Recently there have been auctions specifically devoted to car mascots; Christie's, the London auctioneers, held seven such sales at their South Kensington sale-room between June 1975 and March 1977.

Mascots are not always easy to recognize; any object of metal, glass, wood or even porcelain, can be mounted on the front of cars. Similarly objects that were originally made as mascots can now be found converted into bibelots, paperweights, book-ends, ashtrays, and sometimes lamps. Apart from using the judgement gained by experience, it is often possible to identify a mascot by simple deduction. An object which has to be fixed on a radiator cap must be sturdy and requires a fairly wide bolt in its base. Any small bronze statuette with a slight base or a small hole by which it is fixed is probably not a car mascot.

211.
'Faucon', signed
'R. Lalique'.
France, late 1920s.
Glass, $6\frac{1}{4}$ in
(16 cm).

212. The cat and the moon, signed
'Mercier'. France, early 1920s. Silver-
plated bronze, $4\frac{1}{4}$ in (11 cm).

will obviously post-date the introduction of that type of aircraft.

Stylistic and technical features also
help in dating mascots. For example, on
American cars the radiator cap was
placed inside the bonnet in the early
1930s, so if an American mascot is fixed
to a real radiator cap it antedates this.
In Europe this alteration took place later.
Mascots became more streamlined as
years went by, reflecting the increasingly
aerodynamic shape of cars, so the larger
and more upright the mascot the earlier
it probably is. Also, the finish on mass-
produced mascots has deteriorated over
the years; for example, two apparently
identical greyhounds, perhaps even made
from the same mould, may have different
dates. The chrome plate on the later one
would be much brighter and details such

213. A grinning cat. U.K., 1911. Nickel-
plated bronze, 6 in (15 cm).

Similarly, figures balancing on one foot
with no other support are probably not
mascots, although occasionally a custom
mascot will be made by reinforcing a
statuette and fitting it on to a radiator
cap. Frequently antique dealers them-
selves do not know, and will sell mascots
as mere decorative objects, and vice
versa.

The dates of mascots can also be
deduced. They were generally made of a
metal that was the same colour as the
radiator grille. Thus, in chronological
order, mascots appeared in brass, silver,
bronze, nickel and later on in chromium
plating and glass: the last two materials
were introduced at the end of the 1920s.
Also most custom mascots are early,
so, if several examples are known the
mascot is probably from a later period.
Certain subjects can be ascribed to
specific periods, for instance lucky mascots were mostly made in the first decade
of the century, and patriotic mascots
during World War I. Model aeroplanes

as the seam from the cast will probably be more crude. Some glass mascots such as Lalique's figures of animals, are still produced today as paperweights. Again, an original can be identified by the finish, which on early Lalique glass was always done by hand, and by the signature which is now in a more modern script.

Mascots vary greatly in value according to their design, rarity and condition. In some cases a common mascot such as the Jaguar can be bought more cheaply in a shop or at auction than if ordered from the manufacturer's parts department. Certain company mascots, particularly Rolls Royce's 'Spirit of Ecstasy', the Minerva's head of a goddess and the Hispano-Suiza stork have always been sought after, today as in the 1920s when they first appeared. However, the highest prices are paid for glass mascots. Most custom created mascots fetch high prices, especially when their origins are documented, and when they are signed by a known artist. In each of the seven car mascot auctions held since June 1975,

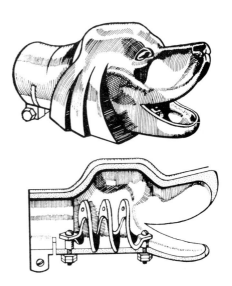

215. 'Woofer', a mascot fixed on exhaust pipes. U.K., 1934. Aluminium.

between one and two hundred mascots have been offered for sale. At all of these some lots were sold inexpensively; common company and fantasy mascots of late date fetched between £5 and £15 ($8.50 to $25). The highest prices were always for glass mascots, ranging from £250 to £450 ($420 to $750).

It is normal for the more sought after mascots to cost more if sold by a retail dealer such as an antique shop. Some fashionable dealers' earlier Lalique glass mascots can be priced at as much as £1,000 to £1,500 ($1,700 to $2,600).

## TAILPIECE

Not all car mascots were designed to precede the driver as a figurehead at the front of his car. Though never particularly successful, some ingenious designer thought up the exhaust-pipe mascot. Advertised as enhancing appearance and improving the sound of exhaust pipes on sports cars, highly polished, aluminium heads of greyhounds, crocodiles, and eagles were available.

214. The 'Courtesy Cat' made by Triangle. U.K., 1934.

# Bibliography

**Magazines**

*Antique Collecting*. Vol. x, No. 6, Oct. 1975.

*Antique Motor News.*

*Automobile Quarterly*. Vol. v, No. 1, 1966.

*Automobile Quarterly*. Vol. x, No. 3, 1972.

*Car Classics.*

*Connaissance des Arts*. April 1977.

*L'Automobiliste, le revue de l'amateur.* No. 10, July/August 1968.

*Special Interest Autos.*

*Thoroughbred and Classic Cars.*

**Books**

*Al Sweigert's Antique Auto Photo Album.* Vol. i, 'The Thirties'. Cleveland 1972.

*American Cars of the 1930s.* Frederick Warne & Co. London and New York 1971.

*American Cars of the 1940s.* Frederick Warne & Co. London and New York 1972.

*American Cars of the 1950s.* Frederick Warne & Co. London and New York 1973.

*Autoamerica*: Ant Farm. E. P. Dutton & Co. New York 1976.

*British Cars in the Early 30s.* Frederick Warne & Co. London 1973.

*Cadillac—The Complete Seventy Year History*: M. D. Henry. The Automobile Quarterly Publications, Princeton 1973.

*Car Badges of the World*: T. Nicholson. Cassell & Co. London 1970.

*Cinquantaine de l'Exposition de 1925.* Catalogue. Musée des Arts Décoratifs, Paris 1976–77.

*Complete Encyclopedia of Motorcars, 1885 to the Present*: G. N. Georgano (Ed.). Ebury Press, London 1973.

*Fifty Years of Lincoln-Mercury*. George H. Damman. Crest Line Publishing, Glen Ellyn, Illinois.

*Fit for the Chase, Cars and the Movies*: R. Lee. Th. Yoseloff, London 1969.

*Gotta Sing Gotta Dance*: G. Korbal. Hamlyn, London and New York 1971.

*L'Art et l'Automobile*: H. Poulain. La Clefs du Temps, Paris 1975.

*Les Années 25.* Catalogue. Musée des Arts Décoratifs, Paris 1966.

*Luxury and Thoroughbred Cars in Profile.* Profile Publications, Windsor 1967.

*Poiret*: P. White. Studio Vista, London 1973.

*Rolling Sculpture*: G. Buehrig & W. Jackson. Haessner, Newfoundland, New Jersey 1975.

*Rolls Royce, The History of the Car.* Martin Bennet. Arco Inc., New York 1974.

*Special Interest American Cars 1930–1960.* Petersen, Los Angeles 1975.

*The Busby Berkeley Book.* Thames and Hudson, London 1973.

*The Fun of Old Cars*: B. Stubenrauch. Dodd Mead & Co. New York 1971.

*The World of Art Deco.* Minneapolis Institute of Arts, Minneapolis 1971.

*The V-12 Hispano-Suiza.* No. 3. Profile Publications, Windsor.

*The 8- & 12-cylinder Packards, 1923–1942.* No. 94. Profile Publications, Windsor.

*Veteran and Vintage Cars in Profile.* Profile Publications, Windsor 1967.

# Index

Page numbers in *italic* refer to illustrations